JAMES DEAN

★ ★ ★ ★ ★ ★ ★ ★ ★ ★ ★ ★ ★ ★

POP CULTURE LEGENDS

JAMES DEAN

★ ★

ALAN SCHROEDER

CHELSEA HOUSE PUBLISHERS

New York ★ Philadelphia

CHELSEA HOUSE PUBLISHERS

EDITORIAL DIRECTOR Richard Rennert
EXECUTIVE MANAGING EDITOR Karyn Gullen Browne
EXECUTIVE EDITOR Sean Dolan
COPY CHIEF Robin James
PICTURE EDITOR Adrian G. Allen
ART DIRECTOR Robert Mitchell
MANUFACTURING DIRECTOR Gerald Levine
PRODUCTION COORDINATOR Marie Claire Cebrián-Ume

POP CULTURE LEGENDS
SENIOR EDITOR Kathy Kuhtz Campbell

Staff for **JAMES DEAN**
COPY EDITOR Nicole Greenblatt
EDITORIAL ASSISTANT Kelsey Goss
PICTURE RESEARCHER Lisa Kirchner
SERIES DESIGN Basia Niemczyc
SENIOR DESIGNER Rae Grant
COVER ILLUSTRATION Richard Leonard

3 5 7 9 8 6 4

Library of Congress Cataloging-in-Publication Data

Alan Schroeder.
James Dean/Alan Schroeder.
p. cm.—(Pop culture legends)
Includes bibliographical references and index.
Summary: A biography of the actor who died in a car accident at the
age of twenty-four and is known for his roles in "East of Eden" and
"Rebel Without a Cause."
ISBN 0-7910-2326-5
    0-7910-2351-6 (pbk.)
1. Dean, James, 1931–1955—Juvenile literature. 2. Motion picture
actors and actresses—United States—Biography—Juvenile literature.
[1. Dean, James, 1931–1955. 2. Actors and actresses.] I. Title. II.
Series.
PN2287.D33S37 1994   93-17708
791.43′028′092—dc20   CIP
[B]   AC

FRONTISPIECE: James Dean
was virtually canonized after
his death. The fans who
adored him understood and
identified with his anger, his
confusion, and his feeling of
always being an outsider.

Contents ★ ★ ★ ★ ★ ★ ★ ★ ★ ★ ★ ★ ★ ★ ★ ★ ★ ★

A Reflection of Ourselves

Leeza Gibbons

I ENJOY A RARE PERSPECTIVE on the entertainment industry. From my window on popular culture, I can see all that sizzles and excites. I have interviewed legends who have left us, such as Bette Davis and Sammy Davis, Jr., and have brushed shoulders with the names who have caused a commotion with their sheer outrageousness, like Boy George and Madonna. Whether it's by nature or by design, pop icons generate interest, and I think they are a mirror of who we are at any given time.

Who are *your* heroes and heroines, the people you most admire? Outside of your own family and friends, to whom do you look for inspiration and guidance, as examples of the type of person you would like to be as an adult? How do we decide who will be the most popular and influential members of our society?

You may be surprised by your answers. According to recent polls, you will probably respond much differently than your parents or grandparents did to the same questions at the same age. Increasingly, world leaders such as Winston Churchill, John F. Kennedy, Franklin D. Roosevelt, and evangelist Billy Graham have been replaced by entertainers, athletes, and popular artists as the individuals whom young people most respect and admire. In surveys taken during each of the past 15 years, for example, General Norman Schwarzkopf was the only world leader chosen as the number-one hero among high school students. Other names on the elite list joined by General Schwarzkopf included Paula Abdul, Michael Jackson, Michael Jordan, Eddie Murphy, Burt Reynolds, and Sylvester Stallone.

More than 30 years have passed since Canadian sociologist Marshall McLuhan first taught us the huge impact that the electronic media has had on how we think, learn, and understand—as well as how we choose our heroes. In the 1960s, Pop artist Andy Warhol predicted that there would soon come a time when every American would be famous for 15 minutes. But if it is easier today to achieve Warhol's 15 minutes of fame, it is also much harder to hold on to it. Reputations are often ruined as quickly as they are made.

And yet, there remain those artists and performers who continue to inspire and instruct us in spite of changes in world events, media technology, or popular tastes. Even in a society as fickle and fast moving as our own, there are still those performers whose work and reputation endure, pop culture legends who inspire an almost religious devotion from their fans.

Why do the works and personalities of some artists continue to fascinate us while others are so quickly forgotten? What, if any, qualities do they share that enable them to have such power over our lives? There are no easy answers to these questions. The artists and entertainers profiled in this series often have little more in common than the enormous influence that each of them has had on our lives.

Some offer us an escape. Artists such as actress Marilyn Monroe, comedian Groucho Marx, and writer Stephen King have used glamour, humor, or fantasy to help us escape from our everyday lives. Others present us with images that are all too recognizable. The uncompromising realism of actor and director Charlie Chaplin and folk singer Bob Dylan challenges us to confront and change the things in our world that most disturb us.

Some offer us friendly, reassuring experiences. The work of animator Walt Disney and late-night talk show host Johnny Carson, for example, provides us with a sense of security and continuity in a changing world. Others shake us up. The best work of composer John Lennon and actor James Dean will always inspire their fans to question and reevaluate the world in which they live.

It is also hard to predict the kind of life that a pop culture legend will lead, or how he or she will react to fame. Popular singers Michael Jackson

and Prince carefully guard their personal lives from public view. Other performers, such as popular singer Madonna, enjoy putting their private lives before the public eye.

What these artists and entertainers do share, however, is the rare ability to capture and hold the public's imagination in a world dominated by mass media and disposable celebrity. In spite of their differences, each of them has somehow managed to achieve legendary status in a popular culture that values novelty and change.

The books in this series examine the lives and careers of these and other pop culture legends, and the society that places such great value on their work. Each book considers the extraordinary talent, the stubborn commitment, and the great personal sacrifice required to create work of enduring quality and influence in today's world.

As you read these books, ask yourself the following questions: How are the careers of these individuals shaped by their society? What role do they play in shaping the world? And what is it that so captivates us about their lives, their work, or the images they present?

Hopefully, by studying the lives and achievements of these pop culture legends, we will learn more about ourselves.

★ 1 ★ Homecoming

In January 1955, James Dean was invited to a small party in Hollywood, California, where he met Dennis Stock, a 26-year-old photographer whose work had appeared in *Life* magazine. During their conversation, Dean happened to mention that he was an actor. Modestly, he added that he had recently completed work on his first film, *East of Eden*. Then as now, Hollywood was full of unknown actors, and Stock assumed that Dean had a small part in the movie.

Later that week, Stock attended a sneak preview of *East of Eden* at a theater in Santa Monica. As the credits began to roll, he was startled to see that Dean was no bit player—he was, in fact, the star of the picture. Sitting in the darkened theater, watching the story unfold, Stock was mesmerized by the intensity of Dean's acting. It contained a powerful and disturbing quality he had rarely seen before. It occurred to him, when the film ended, that Dean was typical of the new breed of American actors—men such as Marlon Brando and Montgomery Clift, who were not afraid to reveal their weaknesses or express their most intimate emotions. On-screen, they held nothing back.

In 1954, James Dean starred in *East of Eden,* the first of three films he would make for Warner Brothers. "Jimmy had the patience of a farmer when he was working," said one Hollywood writer. "It was serious business for him. It was like getting in the crops."

By the time he left the theater, Stock was determined to photograph Dean. "I saw an awkwardness of purity there that I wanted to capture," he said. "I wanted to get to the roots of that earthy quality he had." Stock's experience told him that it would be pointless to assemble a typical collection of "glamour" shots. Instead, he decided to attempt something more ambitious: a full-scale, black-and-white photographic essay that he hoped would reveal the inner man.

Stock shared his idea with Dean, who was eager to cooperate. To make the project unique, Stock suggested they shoot the photos not in Hollywood, but in the two places that meant the most to Dean: New York City, where he had become an actor, and Fairmount, Indiana, where he had been raised as a boy. Though *East of Eden* would not be released until March, the editors at *Life* agreed that it was an interesting concept, and in early February the two men flew to New York to begin the layout.

According to one biographer, Dean saw the trip as "more than just a visit with friends and family. . . . [It was] an opportunity to present his image to the world and redefine it for himself." With Stock at his side, Dean returned to all the spots in New York that had figured prominently in his past—places like Cromwell's Drugstore, a favorite hangout for unemployed actors, and the Cort Theater, where he had appeared in his first Broadway play, *See the Jaguar.*

In a more somber mood, Dean pointed out the Iroquois Hotel, where he once lived in a dingy, depressing room for $90 a month. He also visited the Actors Studio, where, under the watchful eye of Lee Strasberg, he had learned to perfect his art. The toughest and most agonizing days of Dean's life had been spent in New York; nevertheless, it was a city he deeply loved. Los Angeles was nice, in a bland sort of way, but it was in New York that James Dean felt most alive.

Stock realized early on that his subject wanted to be photographed in a certain way. In many shots, for instance, Dean deliberately took off his glasses. He knew this would give him a leaner, sexier edge, but it also revealed an underlying fatigue. Dean was an insomniac— "the worst I've ever met," according to Stock—and in many of the New York photos, dark, puffy circles can be observed under his eyes. Dean was only 24, but already his night-owl life-style was beginning to take its toll.

Every once in a while, Dean would strike a pose that, in Stock's opinion, looked flat and artificial. When this

Dean agreed to allow Dennis Stock (right) to photograph him for an in-depth essay to be published in *Life* magazine. Stock said that when he met Dean at a Hollywood party, "I really didn't know who he was. But once I saw that beanfield scene [in *East of Eden*], I knew he was going to be a really big star."

happened, Stock said, he would have to let Dean "go through a lot of nonsense until he relaxed and became spontaneous. Then I took photos which I thought were revealing of his true character."

Dean's spontaneity expressed itself in different ways. One afternoon, on a whim, he walked into a furniture store, reappearing moments later in the large display window, where he sat down in an armchair. He was hoping to attract a curious crowd, but on this occasion, only a handful of people peered into the window. Another time, to get attention, he dragged a chair into the middle of a busy street and sat down. This time, the results were more gratifying—he caused a major traffic jam, complete with cursing drivers and blaring horns.

Some of Stock's most interesting photos were of Dean interacting with the passersby on the sidewalks of New York. "He had a great natural curiosity about people," said Stock, ". . . and I was forever amazed at the oddities he would stumble on to." Dean had always had an unusually close rapport with children, and one day he spotted two little girls standing in a doorway. One of them was clutching something in her hand. When Dean asked what it was, the girl happily held out her prize: a severed chicken head. Stock was fortunate to capture the moment on film; it was, in many ways, a typical encounter for Dean, combining elements both childlike and strangely surreal.

Whenever he was in New York, Dean stayed at his top-floor apartment on West Sixty-eighth Street. In this intimate setting, Stock photographed whatever he thought the readers of *Life* might find interesting. The tiny apartment, which resembled a college dorm room, contained, among other things, a phonograph, numerous record albums, a tool kit, a pair of bongo drums, and several ink drawings tacked to the wall. The most unusual

Dean poses as a matador. According to one friend, Christine White, Dean "loved bullfighting. The sport did a lot for him in terms of quelling fear. He believed that if you could face a live bull in a bull ring with people watching and hollering, a theater audience would certainly seem tame by comparison."

object in the room was a blood-spattered matador's cape, which Dean had acquired years earlier on a trip to Tijuana, Mexico.

Stock did not know if Dean had ever seen a bullfight, "but he played a lot with that cape—fantasized, I suppose. There was something bull-like about Jimmy—testy, untamed, aggressive." (After the release of *East of Eden, Time* magazine also picked up on Dean's animal-like aura: "He has the presence of a young lion and the same sense of danger about him.")

Before leaving the apartment, Stock photographed Dean's collection of books, which included everything from children's classics to Shakespeare to philosophy. Dean also owned a profusion of how-to books: *How To Etch, How To Sail, Learn Chess Fast.* As a rule, he was too impatient to finish any book he started, but he liked to read, nevertheless. He believed that it was important for him to continually add to his store of knowledge.

Dean, dressed in a pair of tights, is being assisted by a dance teacher during a class in New York. Dancing was only one of Dean's many interests.

16

The trip to Fairmount resulted in a number of interesting photos, including this one that Dennis Stock entitled *Tintype with Sow*.

"An actor should know a little about many things," he once said. "He must do more than project his own personality on the screen. He should represent a cross section of many phases of life. The best way to succeed in this is to learn as much as possible about people and their pursuits. . . . I know I feel more alive when I am trying to master something new."

While in New York, Dean set aside time for a number of his favorite activities. Dressed in a pair of tights, he attended a dance class at the studio of famed choreographer Katherine Dunham. He also participated in a jam session with musician Cyril Jackson, who had taught

17

Dean to play the bongo drums. Though Stock had known Dean only a short while, he sensed that his friend's passion for the bongos had more to do with the particular sound they made "than in the instrument itself; drums, motorcycles, sports cars—all vibrated with a powerful sound to which he responded." Stock's observation was extremely perceptive. Dean loved to make noise—not to annoy others, but to prove to himself that he was young and alive and capable of having fun.

After a week in New York, Dean and Stock flew to Indianapolis, Indiana. From there they took a bus to the rural town of Fairmount, where Dean's aunt and uncle were waiting at the bus station. Marcus and Ortense Winslow were extremely proud of their talented nephew. Like many people in Fairmount, they were following his career closely, especially his TV appearances.

"We had to buy television sets as soon as he began getting parts in programs," said his grandmother, Emma Dean. "Marcus and Ortense had one of the first sets around here, and then Charlie and I got one. The old grapevine got going every time Jimmy was on 'Lux' or 'Studio One'. . . . They'd announce it in school and the neighbors would come streaming in to watch."

After the hectic pace of New York, Dean was glad to be back in Fairmount. The first thing he did was change into a pair of overalls, comfortable boots, and a chino jacket. With Stock following behind, he visited the pigpen, where he was photographed standing next to an enormous, 700-pound hog. (Stock later titled the picture *Tintype with Sow*.) In another photo, Dean can be spotted in the pasture playing the bongos before an audience of appreciative, if bewildered, cattle.

As he had done in New York, Dean returned to the places in Fairmount that revealed something of his origins. One chilly morning, he and Stock paid a visit to Park Cemetery, where generations of Dean's relatives were buried. They also dropped by Marvin Carter's Cycle Shop, where, years earlier, Dean had purchased his first motorbike. On February 14, Dean was invited to the Sweetheart's Ball at Fairmount High, where he was surrounded by excited teenagers asking for autographs.

A seemingly impromptu visit to Hunt's Furniture Store on Main Street resulted in the most notorious of Stock's photos. Mischievously, Dean led the way to a back room, where a number of bronze caskets were on display. After making sure that the coast was clear, he pulled off his boots and climbed into one of the open coffins. He then asked Stock to take a picture, explaining that actress Sarah Bernhardt had often been photographed in this fashion. Besides, he added, he had always wondered what it felt like to be in a coffin. Reluctantly, Stock snapped the shutter, hoping it would put an end to Dean's ghastly curiosity.

But Dean was just getting started. With his typically perverse sense of humor, he began to assume a variety of poses—sitting up, lying down, folding his hands across his chest in a pious imitation of death. Then, to Stock's horror, he gripped the lid of the coffin and pulled it down over him. Like a macabre jack-in-the-box, he then sprang back up, giggling. "When the lid's shut," he said, "it squashes your nose."

Someone at Hunt's must have been spying: Within days the story of Jimmy Dean fooling around in the coffin had become a local scandal. When Marcus Winslow was told what his nephew had done, he shrugged good-naturedly. He and his wife, Ortense, had long ago given up trying to guess what crazy stunt Jimmy would pull next.

After he had returned to Los Angeles, Stock tried to make sense of Dean's bizarre behavior: "It frightened me, and I know it frightened him. He was afraid, but his way of dealing with that fear was to make fun of it, to taunt

Dean plays the bongos at Fairmount High's Valentine's Day dance in February 1955. "[Jimmy] brought his bongos home the last time he came back, just after finishing *East of Eden*," said his aunt Ortense, "and he used to peck at them all the time."

it." Stock also believed that by climbing into the coffin, Dean was trying in some way to feel close to his mother, who had died when he was nine years old. It was a loss from which he had never recovered.

One night, after the Winslows had gone to bed, Dean went to the bookshelf and pulled out a copy of the collected poems of James Whitcomb Riley, Indiana's state poet. Sitting at the kitchen table, cigarette in hand, he read aloud one of his favorite poems, "We Must Get Home." Stock was moved by the reading: "I could feel Jimmy's love of Riley's poems coming through with every word he spoke."

Emotionally, the trip home was important to Dean, but in the long run, it was far more important to the

Winslows, because it was the last time their nephew returned to Fairmount. Seven months later, on September 30, Dean was killed in a car crash on a lonely stretch of highway near Cholame, California. His premature death, and the worldwide hysteria that accompanied it, deeply stunned the residents of Fairmount.

"None of us will ever forget that last family reunion we had with Jimmy," said his grandmother, Emma. ". . . While we're not ones to do much lollygagging around, kissing and hugging each other, it does seem that whenever we're going to be separated . . . we all have tears running down our faces."

Dennis Stock's photo essay appeared in the March 7, 1955, issue of *Life*. Of the hundreds of pictures Stock had taken, there was one that pleased him the most. It was a simple shot of Dean, wearing a camel-hair cap, standing in the driveway of his uncle's farm. His childhood dog, Tuck, stands a few feet behind him, but his head is turned in the opposite direction, away from Dean. The atmosphere of the photo is chilly, slightly surreal, and poignant in its sense of loneliness.

"We were both saddened by the end of the week," remembered Stock, "and I think that we both knew that Jimmy would never come home again. We both recognized that life would never be the same for him there, and that the trip was really a nostalgic farewell to his origins."

2 Indiana Boyhood

James Byron Dean was born on the morning of February 8, 1931, in the industrial town of Marion, Indiana. His mother, Mildred, refused to be taken to the hospital, telling her husband, Winton, that she preferred to deliver the baby at home. It was Mildred's firstborn, and she developed an immediate attachment to her son, rocking him tenderly in her arms and showering him with soft words of affection. A friend warned her that perhaps she was giving young Jimmy too much attention, but Mildred's answer was firm: "He's all that I have, and I love him."

Jimmy was a happy, good-natured toddler, with blue eyes, nimble fingers, and soft, almost feminine features. His grandmother thought he looked like a china doll. Jimmy also had an unusually inquisitive mind. "He had to try everything," said his father, Winton, "and he soon outgrew most of the toys we bought him. He always seemed to be getting ahead of himself."

At the time of his son's birth, Winton was working as a dental technician at the Veterans Administration Hospital in Marion. In 1936, when Jimmy was five, Winton was transferred to another veterans' hospital in Los Angeles,

Dean (kneeling, center) poses for a photograph with his Fairmount High baseball team. According to drama coach Adeline Nall, Jimmy "had this tremendous energy—joined every team the school had even though he was a little fella—and he was always busy with one club or another."

Baby Jimmy appears here in a 1931 photograph with his mother, Mildred, and father, Winton. His grandmother Emma Dean said Jimmy had the features "of a china doll, and the complexion of a ripe apple. Almost too dainty for a boy."

California. The Deans were distressed at having to leave their relatives behind, but the Great Depression left them no choice. More than 10 million Americans were out of work and Winton felt he had to take whatever job was offered. Reluctantly, he and Mildred packed their belongings and the Dean family headed west.

Upon arriving in California, they rented a small cottage in Santa Monica, an oceanfront town not far from Los Angeles. Mildred knew that before long Jimmy would have to begin school, but she was reluctant to cut the apron strings. She loved her son dearly, and they spent a great deal of time together.

With Jimmy seated on her lap, Mildred read aloud her favorite stories and poems, instilling in her son an early appreciation for the arts. She made sure that Jimmy learned how to draw, play the violin, and tap-dance. She encouraged him to use his imagination and, to develop his acting potential, she built a simple theater out of cardboard. Using dolls as miniature actors, she and Jimmy would make up little skits, which they would sometimes perform for Winton when he returned home from the hospital. It was an extremely close and satisfying relationship for both mother and son, one that relied heavily on affection and a rich fantasy life.

By the time Jimmy was ready to start school, he was showing signs of becoming a strong-willed, even obstinate, child. When his father ordered him to do something, he often refused to obey. "Spankings didn't help. . . ." remembered Winton. "And you couldn't bribe him. But you could always reason with him, or appeal to his better instincts. He was that way even when he grew to manhood."

Jimmy entered the first grade in September 1937, but he did not like going to school. He missed his mother and, to make matters worse, the other children teased him about his violin lessons, his midwestern accent, and his unusual middle name, Byron. On the playground, Jimmy insisted that his name was Deanie, but no one listened. Every afternoon, he would wait impatiently for the moment when he could leave the classroom and return to the safe and comforting arms of his mother.

Jimmy's greatest source of pleasure was something called the "wishing game." At night, before going to bed, he would write a wish on a piece of paper, which he would tuck under his pillow. Later, after Jimmy was asleep, Mildred would tiptoe into his room, read the wish, and do her best to make it come true.

In September 1939, Mildred began to complain of pains in her stomach. X rays revealed that she was suffering from cancer of the uterus. The doctors told Winton that his wife could not be saved. He immediately wrote to his mother in Indiana, asking her to come to Santa

When Jimmy was five, he and his family moved to Santa Monica, California. In 1939, when Mildred became seriously ill, Winton found it difficult to explain to Jimmy what was happening. "Jim and I—we'd never had that closeness," Winton admitted. "And my Jim is a tough boy to understand."

Monica to help him through the crisis. Years later, Emma Dean recalled the incident for *Photoplay* magazine: "I'll never forget the day the letter came telling us that Mildred, who was so young and lovely, wouldn't get well. I took the letter to our doctor and he judged I'd be in California about six to eight weeks. I was gone seven to the day."

Sadly, Winton had never developed a close relationship with his son, and he found it difficult to explain to Jimmy that his mother was dying. Naturally, the boy was devastated by the news, but he accepted it in silence, trying desperately to fight back his tears. "Even as a child," Winton remembered, "[Jimmy] wasn't much to talk about things close to him. He never liked to talk about his hurts."

Mildred Dean died on the afternoon of July 14, 1940. During the weeks and months that followed, Jimmy experienced a variety of emotions, including anger, frustration, and a lingering sense of guilt. It is not uncommon for young children to believe that, in some peculiar way, they are responsible for the death of their parent—that if only they had behaved better, the tragedy might have been averted. Nine-year-old Jimmy fell into this psychological trap, one that would cripple him emotionally for the rest of his life.

"Jimmy had a terrible anger for his mother. . . ." said one of his closest friends, Barbara Glenn. "He'd loved her desperately and she left him. I think it had a profound effect on him. And he expressed it in terms of his art."

Mildred's illness had left Winton heavily in debt. After discussing the situation with his mother, he decided to send Jimmy back to Indiana to live with Marcus and Ortense Winslow (Ortense was Winton's older sister). Emma Dean agreed it was a sensible solution. The Winslows, she later explained to an interviewer, "are wise and gentle and have a great gift for loving. Theirs is like a Quaker home should be. You never hear a harsh word. Best of all, they are happy as well as good—and that's what Jimmy needed most after the shock of losing his mother."

On July 16, 1940, Jimmy and his grandmother returned by train to Indiana. The coffin containing Mildred's body was carried in the baggage car, and at every stop, Jimmy ran back to make sure it was still aboard.

After the sunwashed beauty of Santa Monica, the flat plains of Grant County, Indiana, must have come as a shock to young Jimmy. According to one writer, the

Hoosier landscape was visually harsh, "a place pared down to the rind and as plain and unadorned" as the Quakers who had settled there many years before.

Marcus and Ortense Winslow lived on a farm outside the town of Fairmount, 40 miles north of Indianapolis. Unselfishly, they welcomed Jimmy into their home, raising him as if he were their own child. (The Winslows already had one daughter, Joan, who was five years older than Jimmy. Another child, Marcus "Markie," Jr., was born in 1943.) Marcus and Ortense understood the pain that Jimmy was going through and, to the best of their ability, they helped him adjust to the tragic loss of his mother and the enforced separation from his father.

Originally, Winton had planned to retrieve his son as soon as he was financially stable, but Jimmy ended up spending a total of nine years in the quiet, simple community of Fairmount. For the most part, his adolescence was happy and uneventful. He rode his bicycle through the meadow, taught himself to swim in a nearby creek, and played hide-and-seek in the barn with his cousins. After school, he helped his aunt and uncle with the chores, milking the cows and collecting eggs from the henhouse. His grandparents, Charlie and Emma Dean, owned a farm on the other side of Fairmount, and Jimmy enjoyed visiting them, his dog Tuck tagging along at his heels.

While living in Santa Monica, Jimmy had been a frail child, prone to nosebleeds and occasional bouts of anemia. He was also small for his age and extremely nearsighted. In Fairmount, his condition began to improve. The chores he performed daily built up his strength and he suffered no more episodes of anemia.

Within a year or so, he had become an athletic, almost hyperactive, child with an abundance of youthful energy. Recognizing this, Marcus installed a trapeze in the barn and each night, after supper, he gave his nephew gymnastic lessons. (On one occasion, Jimmy crashed into a pipe and knocked out his front teeth. His father, Winton, made him a dental bridge, which Jimmy wore for the rest of his life.)

Like most farm boys, Jimmy involved himself in various 4-H projects. During his first year with the Winslows, he raised a brood of baby chicks; later, he bottle-fed a piglet, which became his pet. He also raised cattle, taking a blue ribbon one year at the Grant County Fair.

"Jimmy was just like any other kid who grew up in this town," said Marcus. "He played baseball, went to Sunday Meeting at Back Creek Quaker Church and did his chores on the farm. Used to tag around after me opening gates so I wouldn't have to get off the tractor."

After the death of his mother, young Jimmy was sent to live with his aunt and uncle, the Winslows, on their farm in Fairmount. By the time he was 17, Jimmy had broken the Grant County pole-vaulting record, even though he was only five feet eight inches tall.

The Winslows went out of their way to make Jimmy happy. In the winter, Marcus strung up electric lights in the trees so Jimmy and Joan could ice-skate on the frozen pond after dark. In the fall, there were hayrides and barn parties where the children danced and bobbed for apples. Upon learning of her nephew's interest in the arts, Ortense arranged for Jimmy to take drawing and dancing lessons, and he spent many enjoyable hours practicing the clarinet and drums.

"Jimmy had all the fun that could be had and then some," remembered Ortense. "He put more living into every day than anyone I ever saw."

As a student, Jimmy failed to distinguish himself. This was perhaps due to a reading problem and a tendency to daydream. One teacher, India Nose, said that sometimes Jimmy was "moody, and often unexplainably stubborn. He could be forgetful, too, as if he were lost in a daze."

Because he lived outside of town, Jimmy never made many friends, but as one classmate recalled, "He didn't have any enemies either. After a while he settled down like the rest of us, just an average kid, except that sometimes he did what you might call dumb things—stunts, I mean—to attract attention. I'm sure that had something to do with his mother dying like that when he was so young."

The memory of Mildred's death continued to torment Jimmy. More than a decade later, on the set of *Rebel Without a Cause,* he confided to costar Dennis Hopper the grief he experienced as an adolescent. "I used to sneak out of my uncle's house at night and go to her grave," he said, "and I used to cry and cry on her grave—'Mother, why did you leave me? Why did you leave me? I need you. . . . I want you.'"

Ortense Winslow was a practical woman and she tried to minimize her nephew's anguish by keeping him busy. When Jimmy was in the seventh grade, she encouraged him to perform a dramatic monologue for the Women's Christian Temperance Union (WCTU). Jimmy read so well that he was given a prize for his efforts. This spurred him to do more public recitations. The pieces he selected were often gruesome in nature, but as Jimmy admitted, "I won all the medals the WCTU had to offer."

He became such an accomplished speaker that he decided to compete for the Pearl Medal, the highest honor bestowed by the WCTU. The competition piece was called "Bars," a passionate condemnation of the evils of alcohol. Adeline Nall, who taught drama at Fairmount High School, thought it was an inappropriate monologue for a youngster to perform. Nevertheless, when Jimmy asked for her help, she was glad to assist. For several days, she coached him at the high school, teaching him how to stand, how to project his voice, and how to use gestures effectively.

Jimmy worked hard, but on the night of the contest, his recitation was not a success. His one prop, a chair, was taken away just as he was about to go on. Unnerved, he forgot his lines, stopped cold and, much to his aunt's embarrassment, walked offstage. "I was sure then what I had suspected all along," said Ortense. "You couldn't make James Dean do things he didn't want to do. He had a mind all of his own."

Though Jimmy did not win the Pearl Medal, Adeline Nall continued to take an interest in him. She sensed that he had acting ability and, to help bring it out, she arranged for him to appear in school plays, first in small parts, then in larger, more challenging roles. Jimmy and Adeline got along well, and under her thoughtful coaching, he became a talented and enthusiastic actor.

By this time, Jimmy had also developed a passion for sports. Upon entering high school in the fall of 1944, he joined as many teams as he could, doing well in baseball, basketball, and track. He also broke the Grant County

A bespectacled Jimmy balances a basketball in this photograph taken during his high school years. According to actor Dennis Hopper, Jimmy "could barely see four feet in front of him. He thought that it helped him tremendously as an actor because he had to imagine everything that was happening beyond that point."

record for pole vaulting. Always, he pushed himself to the limit, trying to prove to the other boys—and to himself—that he could excel at whatever he set his mind to.

"[Jimmy] was what you would call a clean-cut, all-American type boy," said basketball coach Paul Weaver. "In his movies you see quite a bit of what he actually was—quiet, soft-spoken and reserved."

When Jimmy was a sophomore, Marcus gave him permission to buy a used motorcycle. Driving to and from school, the 16-year-old gradually became obsessed with speed. He loved to feel the wind whipping through his hair, tugging at the sleeves of his jacket. Much to the dismay of his aunt and uncle, Jimmy became a daredevil who loved to take risks, popping wheelies at 40 miles per hour.

"If he'd only fallen once, things might have been different," said Marcus. "Trouble is, he never got hurt. . . . Just one fall off the bike and maybe he'd have been afraid of speed, but he was without fear."

It was during this period that Jimmy became friends with Dr. James DeWeerd, the young, charismatic pastor of Fairmount's Wesleyan church. Like many local boys, Jimmy was fascinated by DeWeerd, a decorated veteran who had seen and experienced more of the world than most people. Jimmy had many long talks with the pastor, during which DeWeerd encouraged him to learn as much as he could. "The more you know how to do," he told Jimmy, "and the more things you experience, the better off you'll be."

To some extent, DeWeerd picked up where Jimmy's mother had left off, exposing the youth to art, poetry, literature, and classical music. Jimmy enjoyed DeWeerd's humorous stories, and the more he listened, the more eager he became to leave Indiana and discover the world for himself. Like a guide, DeWeerd opened up new vistas for Jimmy, who willingly followed.

In the small community of Fairmount, Jimmy was regarded as something of a loner, and he began to use the pastor as a sounding board for his problems. He tried to explain to DeWeerd that he felt like an outsider. He was too restless, he said, to conform to the Quaker life-style, which stressed a reverence for simplicity and traditional family values. DeWeerd told Jimmy not to be ashamed of his difference, but to take pride in it, to wear it as a badge of honor. DeWeerd believed that conformity was a sign of cowardice, a daring thought for a preacher to express in the heart of Quaker country.

As their friendship deepened, Jimmy began to reveal his innermost thoughts, things that he felt he could not

This photograph of Dean as a senior appeared in his high school yearbook. "I don't think [Jimmy] brought a girl [to the Fairmount High senior prom]," said one classmate. "He didn't date a lot during school. Oh, the girls liked him, but I guess he wasn't interested."

discuss with the Winslows. According to DeWeerd, "Jimmy poured out . . . his belief that he must be evil, or his mother would not have died and his father wouldn't have sent him away." The Wesleyan preacher attempted to comfort Jimmy, and the emotional bond that developed between them was extremely close.

In the fall of 1948, Jimmy started his senior year at Fairmount High. By then, he had appeared in a number of plays and was considered one of the school's most outstanding actors. According to Adeline Nall, Jimmy was a perfectionist when it came to the theater: "He wanted everything to be exactly right. He nearly caused a riot by keeping the kids rehearsing one night until nearly midnight. And the next day . . . my goodness, did those parents call the school and raise heck! Even then Jim's attitude was, 'If you want to act, you have to give up everything for your acting.'"

As much as he loved the world of theater, Jimmy was growing increasingly depressed. James DeWeerd had taught him that life was full of possibilities, and now, as graduation approached, Jimmy was anxious to go to New York or Los Angeles to study acting. But hardly anyone in the farming community of Fairmount sympathized with his ambition. As the months wore on, Jimmy could feel himself growing impatient with the people around him, even the Winslows, who had always given him their unconditional love. Like many teenagers, he felt hemmed in and misunderstood.

There was also the matter of his sexuality. Jimmy had dated a handful of girls, but during his senior year, his relationship with James DeWeerd appears to have become physical. Jimmy felt no shame that he had bisexual tendencies, but he must have realized the potential difficulties of the situation. In the 1940s, homosexuality was a subject rarely discussed in public. Many people regarded it as a form of mental illness, and surely Jimmy sensed that if he stayed in Fairmount he would eventually become an object of ridicule or persecution.

As his frustrations continued to mount, his behavior became troublesome and confusing to the Winslows. "We didn't know what was the matter," said Marcus. "He didn't take any more stock in us and refused to help out. We were at wits' end. *He was no longer one of us.*"

3 Striking Out

In the spring of 1949, James Dean played the role of "the mad Russian," Boris Kolenkhov, in a high school production of Thornton Wilder's *You Can't Take It with You*. It was only a small part, but according to Adeline Nall, Dean played it "with all the verve of a veteran."

Soon afterward, he won first place in a statewide speaking competition sponsored by the National Forensic League. His victory entitled him to travel to Longmont, Colorado, for the Nationals. The proud residents of Fairmount immediately started up a fund, raising more than $100 to send Dean and his drama teacher to Longmont.

The piece he selected for the tournament was "The Madman," an excerpt from Charles Dickens's *Pickwick Papers*. Bursting out from behind a curtain, he began his recitation with a blood-curdling scream. The performance that followed was compelling, if melodramatic: "Yes! A Madman's! . . . the blood hissing and tingling through my veins, till the cold dew of fear stood in large drops upon my skin, and my knees knocked together with fright! Ho! Ho! It's a fine thing to be mad!"

In 1950, Dean played the part of Malcolm in UCLA's production of Shakespeare's *Macbeth*. Although he was given a harsh review in the theater department's newsletter, Dean caught the attention of a talent agent who happened to see his performance.

Dean gave the piece everything he had, modulating his voice and movements as the intensity rose and fell. During rehearsals, Nall had warned him that the monologue was running overtime, but Dean had resisted her attempts to trim it. Perhaps for this reason, he did not win the contest; when the prizes were announced, the teenager from Fairmount placed sixth.

Nall was disappointed by the outcome, but she managed to remain optimistic. "I hope this is only the beginning of much more fine work in this field," she told a Longmont newspaper reporter.

Despite his failure to win the competition, Dean returned to Fairmount full of enthusiasm and purpose. He was convinced that if he worked hard he could become a successful actor, and when he broached the subject to his aunt and uncle, they gave him their full support. Whatever he wanted to do was fine with them.

On May 16, 1949, James Dean graduated from Fairmount High. A few weeks later, he packed his bags and boarded a Greyhound bus bound for California. For the past several months, his father had been encouraging him to move west to attend college, and Dean agreed it was a good idea. The University of California at Los Angeles (UCLA) had an outstanding theater department and, before leaving Fairmount, Dean told the local paper that he planned "to take a course in dramatics and fine arts" at UCLA that fall.

After a four-day bus ride, he arrived in Southern California, where he was reunited with his father, whom he had seen only a few times since moving to Fairmount nine years earlier. In 1943, Winton had been drafted into the Army Medical Corps. Two years later, after the war, he had married a woman named Ethel Case. Jim treated his stepmother cordially, but they never developed a close relationship.

To save money, Jim moved into his father's apartment in Santa Monica, but almost immediately they had a disagreement. Winton felt that his 18-year-old son should attend Santa Monica City College—it was close to home and offered a variety of practical courses. Patiently, Jim tried to explain to his father that he had come to California to study acting, but Winton refused to listen. In his opinion, acting was a poor choice for a career. It was too unstable, he said.

After a number of strained conversations, Dean gave in to his father's wishes. In January 1950, he enrolled as a pre-law student at Santa Monica City College. He managed, nevertheless, to squeeze into his schedule as

Acrobats entertain a crowd on Muscle Beach in Santa Monica, California. After graduating from high school, Dean moved to Santa Monica to live with his father.

many theater courses as possible. At that time, the chairwoman of the drama department was Gene Owen. Like Adeline Nall, she spotted Dean's talent immediately and began to give him advice and encouragement.

Years later, reading the countless articles about James Dean that appeared after his death, Owen found it difficult to reconcile the turbulent young man presented in the fan magazines with the accommodating student she had known in Santa Monica.

"Jimmy was not moody, temperamental, unpredictable or rude. . . ." she said. "He was always polite and thoughtful; his enthusiasm for everything that pertained to the theater was boundless."

One day, she asked Dean to read aloud from Edgar Allan Poe's "The Tell-Tale Heart." A masterful story, it chronicles the psychological torment of a man who has murdered his employer and buried the body under the floorboards. During a police interrogation, the half-crazed killer believes his victim's heart is still beating loudly, until, in a frenzy, he confesses his guilt: "Villains! . . . I admit the deed!—tear up the planks! here, here!—it is the beating of his hideous heart!"

As usual, Dean tore into the part, astonishing everyone in the classroom. "He was magnificent," remembered Owen. "But then he always had a spectacular emotion for any scene he played." Later that day, she had Dean read some scenes from Shakespeare's *Hamlet*. His portrayal of the tortured Danish prince affected her deeply. "He had an extraordinary perception of the role," she said, "electrifying and different. I was staggered by his work with the soliloquies."

Winton Dean was not an unreasonable man, and as time passed, he realized that his son's heart was set on acting. In the fall of 1950, he allowed Jim to enroll as a theater arts major at UCLA. To avoid the inconvenience of a daily commute, Jim moved out of his father's small apartment and into a room at Sigma Nu fraternity house.

Gene Owen had advised Jim not to transfer. Academically, she did not think he was ready; nor did she think that he would be able to survive the competitive atmosphere of UCLA's Theater Arts Department. As it turned out, she was correct on both counts. Jim's grades at the university proved to be mediocre and the one important performance he gave disappointed everyone.

The theater department at UCLA planned to produce four plays during the 1950–51 school year. The most ambitious undertaking was a full-scale production of Shakespeare's *Macbeth*. The play, Jim wrote to his aunt and uncle, "will be presented in Royce Hall (seats 1600). After the auditioning of 367 actors and actresses, I came up with a wonderful lead in *Macbeth*, the character being Malcolm (huge part)."

Unfortunately, the role did not suit Dean and his performance was unmemorable. The theater department newsletter gave him a harsh, one-sentence review: "Malcolm (James Dean) failed to show any growth and would have made a hollow king." A talent agent, however, happened to catch Dean's performance and, much to his delight, she agreed to take him on as a client.

Macbeth was the only show in which Dean appeared during his short stay at UCLA. One of his professors, Dr. Walden Boyle, sensed that Dean was unhappy at the school: "I guess the university life was much too slow for him. I got the feeling he wanted to act and nothing more than that, so he didn't take to the rest of the academic requirements."

Dean also had trouble adjusting to life in a fraternity. Because he tended to keep to himself, his frat brothers considered him secretive and unfriendly. Nor were they comfortable with his ambiguous sexuality. A few years later, when questioned point-blank about his sexual preference, Dean's answer was revealing: "Well, I'm certainly not going through life with one hand tied behind my back."

In 1951, however, this sly admission of bisexuality would have been unacceptable to the young men at Sigma Nu. They wanted to know if Dean was attracted to men or women, and to force the issue, they began to tease him about all the "fairies" in the theater department. Finally, Dean let loose and punched one of his frat brothers in the nose. He was promptly ordered to move out.

Forced to find new lodgings in a hurry, he suggested to an acquaintance of his, Bill Bast, that they share an apartment. Bast, a theater arts major at UCLA, was taken aback by the suddenness of the proposal. It sounded like a reasonable idea, however, and within a few days they had located a three-room penthouse apartment in Santa Monica. To pay his share of the rent, Dean found a job parking cars at the CBS radio studio.

Bast was one of the few people who got to know James Dean on an intimate basis. They shared a passion for acting and quickly became close friends. Sometimes, when they could afford it, they went on double dates together. On one such outing, Bast's companion was a young actress named Beverly Wills. At first, Wills thought Dean was a "creep." Then they began to talk about acting. Suddenly, she said, Dean "lit up. He told me how interested he was in the Stanislavsky method, where you not only act out people, but things too." To demonstrate, Dean mimicked the motion of a palm tree in a storm; then, pulling off his jacket, he pretended to be a monkey. "He climbed a big tree," said Wills, "and swung from a high branch. . . . Once in the spotlight, he ate it up and had us all in stitches. . . . The 'creep' turned into the hit of the party."

Between classes, Dean spent his time driving from one Hollywood studio to another, hoping to make a screen test. Religiously, he read the trade papers, circling any ad that sounded promising. He went to auditions and "cattle calls," where he tried to make himself known to producers and casting directors.

Gradually, small jobs began to come his way. First, he appeared in a one-minute commercial for Pepsi-Cola, shot in nearby Griffith Park. After that, he was given a more substantial part in a TV special called "Hill Number One." A religious drama set during the time of Christ, Dean played the part of John the Apostle. The camera picked up some of his nervousness, but it made no difference to the girls at Immaculate Heart High School, who had been required to watch the telecast. They instantly formed a James Dean Appreciation Society—his first fan club.

"Hill Number One" was broadcast on Easter Sunday, 1951. Shortly thereafter, Dean had a falling-out with Bill Bast, who moved out of the Santa Monica apartment. Unable to afford the rent alone, Dean moved in with Rogers Brackett, a witty, 35-year-old advertising executive whom he had met in the parking lot at CBS.

Brackett had many valuable contacts in the industry and was able to get Dean a job on "Alias Jane Doe," a weekly radio program. He also arranged for Dean to appear in his first film, *Fixed Bayonets,* in which he played a bit part as a soldier. "There we were," Dean said, "all crouched down behind this hill, covered with dirt and sweat. . . . I had exactly one

Dean appears here in a wardrobe shot for Universal's Has Anybody Seen My Gal?, a film released in 1952. Dean quickly tired of playing walk-on parts in B movies and decided to move to New York City. "People approach acting differently in New York," he was told by his friend and teacher, James Whitmore.

line. It went: 'It's a rear guard coming back.'" To his disappointment, the line was cut during the final edit.

Dean next appeared in a low-budget comedy, *Sailor Beware* (1951), which starred the popular team of Dean Martin and Jerry Lewis. This time, Dean was given three lines—which also ended up on the cutting-room floor. He was finally allowed to speak in Universal's *Has Anybody Seen My Gal?* (1952), placing a complicated order at a soda fountain: "Hey, Gramps, I'll have a choc malt, heavy on the choc, plenty of milk, four spoons of malt, two scoops of vanilla ice cream, one mixed with the rest and one floating."

It was an amusing bit of dialogue, but Dean quickly became impatient playing walk-on parts in B movies. Like most students at UCLA, he was anxious to tackle a juicy, dramatic role, but the Hollywood studios had nothing to offer him. He was too new, an unknown commodity. He needed to prove himself first.

As autumn approached, the bit parts began to dry up and Dean fell into a deep depression. "I soon learned that it was nothing for Jimmy to run through a whole alphabet of emotions in one evening," said Beverly Wills, whom Dean was now dating. "[He] couldn't get an acting job and he was growing increasingly bitter. I hated to see Jimmy become so blue. When he was happy, there was no one more loveable. When he was depressed, he wanted to die."

In this despondent state, Dean forced himself to continue looking for work. At auditions and casting calls, he kept hearing references to the Actors Studio in New York, where students learned the Stanislavsky method of acting. Out of curiosity, he began to attend a class taught by actor James Whitmore, who belonged to the Studio. Whitmore took an interest in Dean, and occasionally, after class, they would talk about Dean's unsuccessful attempts to find a job.

"I owe a lot to Whitmore," Dean admitted. "I guess you can say he saved me when I got all mixed up. . . . There's always someone in your life who opens up your eyes. For me, that's Whitmore. He made me see myself. He opened me up, gave me the key."

The "key" Dean referred to was Whitmore's suggestion that he leave Los Angeles.

"Stop dissipating your energy and talent," Whitmore said. "Go to New York. There you will find out whether you can take the uncertainty of an actor's life. . . . Learn to study. Learn to act—and above all, act. You get to be an actor by acting."

Dean carefully reviewed his situation. As he saw it, there was no compelling reason to stay and every reason to leave. Thus far, his return to California had been one disappointment after another: his uneasy relationship with his father and stepmother; his classes at UCLA; his poor performance in *Macbeth;* his failure to fit in with the brotherhood at Sigma Nu. He was always in debt and, to make matters worse, his relationship with Beverly Wills had come to a sour conclusion.

In the end, Dean decided that Whitmore was right. If he wanted to be taken seriously as an actor, he needed to go to New York. There, at the Actors Studio, his ability would be put to the test, and he would learn once and for all if he had the talent necessary to become a great artist.

Before leaving Los Angeles, he sought out Beverly Wills to say good-bye. She later recorded Dean's poignant departure. "I kissed him on the cheek, wished him well, and watched him walk down the street," she wrote. "He kicked at some stones like a little boy . . . and he stopped under a lamppost to light a cigarette. Then he squared his shoulders, turned the corner, and was gone."

4 ★ New York: Act One

Excited and a bit fearful, James Dean arrived in New York City in September 1951. His self-confidence had been shaken by his inability to find steady work in Hollywood. He was no longer the hotshot kid impressing the folks back in Fairmount with his recitations. Here, on the grimy sidewalks of New York, he was just another hungry, anonymous actor looking for a job.

Initially, he found the experience of living in a vast metropolis overwhelming. "For the first few weeks," he wrote to the Winslows, "I was so confused that I strayed only a couple of blocks from my hotel off Times Square. I would see three movies a day in an attempt to escape from my loneliness and depression."

Despite the proliferation of theaters in New York, Dean found it impossible to land an acting job. Armed with his portfolio containing black-and-white photos and a short résumé, he went to numerous auditions, only to discover hundreds of young actors all competing for the same role. Gradually, hope turned to discouragement, and discouragement to despair.

In December 1952, Constance Ford, James Dean (center), and Arthur Kennedy appear in the Broadway play *See the Jaguar.* According to one critic, Dean played the part of Wally Wilkins "with sweetness and naïveté that made his tortures singularly poignant."

47

To reduce his living expenses, he moved into a cheap room at the YMCA on West Sixty-third Street. There he spent his time reading or listening to classical records. Dean had always loved music, and during his first months in New York, he became friendly with composer Leonard Rosenman, who would later write the scores for two of Dean's films, *East of Eden* and *Rebel Without a Cause*. Rosenman and his wife, Adele, became very fond of Dean and, sensing his loneliness, frequently invited him to dinner at their spacious apartment on Central Park West.

"Jimmy was really interested in everything. . . ." recalled Adele Rosenman. "He had the ability to absorb from everyone he met something that he could digest and that would later be useful to him as an actor. He discarded the things that were not of use to him."

In November, Dean found an unlikely job to pay the bills. He was hired as a stuntman for the popular television show "Beat the Clock." Week after week, countless Americans tuned in to watch contestants compete for prizes by trying to perform outlandish stunts. It was Dean's job to try out the stunts beforehand, to make sure that they were safe and, indeed, performable.

"What I remember most about Jimmy was his dogged determination never to let anything beat him," said Frank Wayne, one of the show's writers. "[If he] couldn't do a stunt in the lab session, he would stay on his own time doing it over and over again until he finally got it. . . . He had that same determination about becoming a star."

During this period, Dean was introduced to a talent agent named Jane Deacy, who agreed to represent him. Dean had had an agent in California, Isabelle Draesmer, but she had been unable to further his career in any significant way. Deacy was different. She had the contacts and the personal interest in Dean to make things happen.

In February 1952, she arranged for him to make his first New York television appearance, playing a bellhop on the CBS mystery series, "The Web." At that time, New York was the center of the television industry. Each week, more than 30 shows were broadcast live, and at each of the networks there was an insatiable demand for creative talent of all kinds.

According to actor Charlton Heston, "Television provided an opportunity for a whole generation of actors, writers and directors to come through. The studios wouldn't allow any of their contract players or directors to have anything to do with television, so that wiped out a whole colony of people who were willing and able to do it. The theater people wouldn't do it either; they thought it was all rather tacky, and the new medium was left to a bunch of 24-year-olds whose basic qualification was that they were unemployed."

Jane Deacy worked hard for her client, and by midsummer Dean had appeared on half a dozen programs, including "Studio One," "Lux Video Theater," and "Hallmark Summer Theater." He was still an unknown, but he was getting plenty of valuable experience. He was acting, just as James Whitmore had advised him to do.

By this time, Dean was living once again with Rogers Brackett, who had come to New York to direct a radio show. Their relationship had begun to deteriorate, however, and Dean was anxious to find new living arrangements. He wrote to his old roommate, Bill Bast, telling him that life in New York was terrific. Bast was hoping to find work as a television writer and, in the summer of 1952, he moved to the Big Apple.

Dean immediately suggested they find an apartment together. Bast was leery—he knew firsthand how difficult it was to cope with Dean's unpredictable mood swings. When everything was going well, Dean could be a charming, funny, and generous person. Upon experiencing any sort of setback, however, he could become sullen and uncommunicative. To the dismay of his friends, Dean

When Dean moved to New York City in 1951, he rented a hotel room not far from Times Square (pictured here) and he felt insecure. "You have to remember that Jimmy was still something of a hayseed," said actor Frank Corsaro. "Wide-eyed at the whole scene . . . he was totally American apple pie."

would allow himself to become obsessed with images of death and dying.

Nevertheless, Bast needed a place to live, and the same day he arrived in New York, he and Dean moved into a $90-a-month room at the Iroquois Hotel on West Forty-fourth Street. It was an ugly space, painted a depressing gray-green color. They put up with it for a month or two, then decided to move into a brownstone on West Eighty-ninth Street with Dizzy Sheridan, a dancer whom Dean had once dated.

"The night we moved," said Bast, "we were particularly broke. . . . We had between us less than a dollar on which to eat. So, like scavengers, we took all the leftovers

from the refrigerator and made a stew into which Jimmy dumped a half a package of old vermicelli. . . . As we sat eating the mess, not one of us would acknowledge the presence of tiny bugs floating atop the broth. Each of us surreptitiously dipped out the little intruders and continued to eat in silence."

That summer, Dean had the good fortune to be introduced to Lemuel Ayres, who was about to produce a new play on Broadway, *See the Jaguar*. Like the Rosenmans, Ayres and his wife became very fond of Dean, who accompanied them on a boat trip to Cape Cod, Massachusetts, in August. During the week-long cruise, Ayres and Dean talked about the theater in general and *See the Jaguar* in particular. Auditions for the play would not be held for another two months, Ayres said, but he promised to let Dean read for a part.

A few weeks later, while visiting Jane Deacy at her office, Dean happened to meet a young actress named Christine White. He asked her out and, over coffee at Cromwell's Drugstore, he told her about his recent television work. She, in turn, told him that in November she would be auditioning for the Actors Studio. In fact, she had written a short scene that she was planning to use as her audition piece. Dean read the scene, liked it, and in his usual ingratiating way convinced White to allow him to become her partner. They would do the scene together, he said.

Dean and White spent the next five weeks rehearsing and rewriting, trying to make the piece as strong as possible. Years later, White would look back affectionately on their collaboration: "[We] believed that the world was ours and everything was possible. . . . Jimmy told me of his many ambitions: he wanted to fight bulls, he wanted to be a director. . . . He told me about the Indiana farm where he had been raised and his appreciation of land and space. He told me how much he missed his mother, but he did so without any self-pity. He was an all-American boy, sometimes serious, often moody, mostly always driven to succeed."

While Dean and White were putting the finishing touches on their scene, Dean was asked by Lemuel Ayres to audition for *See the Jaguar*. The drama, written by N. Richard Nash, chronicles one day in the life of Wally Wilkins, a simpleton hidden away for years in an abandoned icehouse by his half-crazy mother, who wants to protect her son "from all the meanness of the world." Upon his mother's death, Wally wanders to the nearest town, but finds himself unable to deal with the complications of society. At the end of the play, locked in a steel cage, he has only one wish—to return to the safety of the icehouse.

It was a peculiar and tricky role, and Dean's reading at the first audition was impressive. According to Nash, he "brought a great richness to the part. There are scenes of deep puzzlement, and you have never seen such puzzlement as portrayed by Dean. . . . It was deep down and quite beautiful." Dean's additional readings were equally moving and, to his great relief, he was hired for the part.

Shortly thereafter, on November 12, he and Christine White auditioned for the Actors Studio. The scene that they had prepared took place on an island about to be hit by a hurricane. A young woman running away from her parents has a brief, disturbing encounter with a beach bum. Dean was extremely nervous before the audition, but he and his partner performed well and were complimented afterward by stage and film director Elia Kazan, who was sitting in the audience.

"I have made great strides in my craft," Dean later wrote to the Winslows. "After months of auditioning, I am very proud to announce that I am a member of the Actors Studio, the greatest school of the theater. It houses great people like Marlon Brando, Julie Harris, Arthur

Kennedy, Elia Kazan, . . . Monty Clift and June Havoc. It is the best thing to happen to any actor."

Though Dean felt honored to be admitted to such select company, he had no time to begin attending sessions at the Studio. He was much too busy rehearsing his role in *See the Jaguar,* which opened at the Cort Theater on December 3, 1952. Among those who attended the opening-night performance was actress Mildred Dunnock, who would later work with Dean on a CBS television show. Like most people who saw the play, Dunnock found it awkward and unconvincing. Nevertheless, she was touched by the sincerity of Dean's performance. "He was very bright," she recalled, "with an absolute instinct. He could smell falseness, he could smell artificiality."

After the final curtain, the entire cast went to Sardi's, a popular New York restaurant, to celebrate. Dean knew he had performed well and his mood that evening was ecstatic. "His feet never touched the floor," said Dean's roommate, Dizzy Sheridan. "He just flew from table to table, talking, laughing. I watched people's eyes pouring adulation all over him. . . . I had the feeling that things were starting to move for Jimmy."

Sheridan was right. Though *See the Jaguar* closed after only five performances, it proved to be an important stepping-stone in Dean's career. For the first time, people within the industry began talking about James Dean. Columnists wanted to interview him. Even Metro-Goldwyn-Mayer (MGM) offered to fly him to California for a screen test, but Dean said no. As Jane Deacy had explained to him, he needed to appear in another play first, to prove to the studio heads that he could handle a "mature" part. Like most actors, Dean was impatient to become a star, but he wisely took his agent's advice and waited for the right role to come along.

In the meantime, he turned his attention to the Actors Studio, where he began to attend sessions after the closure

The Russian director Konstantin Stanislavsky (1863–1938) cofounded the Moscow Art Theater and developed a "method" of acting that greatly influenced the work of such American actors as Marlon Brando and James Dean. According to one writer, a Method actor "learns to use his mind, his senses, and his feeling as effectively as he learns to use his body and voice."

of *See the Jaguar*. Founded in 1947 by Elia Kazan and others, it was one of the few places in America where students could learn "the Method," a controversial approach to acting developed earlier in the century by Russian director Konstantin Stanislavsky.

Misunderstood and often ridiculed by outsiders, the Method teaches an actor how to use personal experience to give a truthful performance. In his attempt to rid the Russian theater of what he called "tired cliché," Stanislavsky developed a psychological technique whereby an actor could probe his inner self and remember past emotional incidents (a severe scolding, for instance, or the death of a beloved pet). The feelings thus exposed, according to one writer, could then be harvested "to breathe life into a characterization and performance." Honesty was a key watchword at the Actors Studio. "That you were not being truthful was the worst thing you could be told," said Studio member Frank Corsaro. "That you were acting, not being."

Stanislavsky also believed that before an actor could give a realistic performance, he or she must understand precisely what motivates his or her character to do certain things. This could be accomplished only by studying one's character thoroughly and by imagining how that character would react in circumstances not presented in the play. Stanislavsky not only wanted his actors to treat their characters as if they were real people, he wanted them to carry their characterizations into their private, offstage lives—to lose themselves, in essence, and become somebody else.

In a modified form, the Method was introduced at the Actors Studio in 1948 by Lee Strasberg, who went on to become one of the guiding lights of the American theater. Even more than Stanislavsky, Strasberg encouraged his students to dig deep within themselves, to remember past incidents, and to seize upon the emotions connected with them. Feelings of hurt, betrayal, anger, joy, embarrassment, guilt—all were brought to the surface and explored at the Actors Studio.

Special memory exercises (often involving meditation) were developed to help members get in touch with their private feelings. These emotions—however painful the process of retrieving them—could then be used as building blocks to create a character onstage. "The more an actor knows about *himself*," said Strasberg, "the more he will be able to make use of himself."

Like all actors, those who studied the Method were encouraged to become sharp observers of the human condition. "Is it hard for a fat man to turn his neck?" Stanislavsky would ask. "How does he sit down, stand up? Does he eat and drink in a certain way? . . . Observe fat men in life and try as correctly as possible to reproduce them."

It was a fascinating exercise, and Dean spent hours honing his observational skills. Walking the crowded

Actor and director Lee Strasberg (wearing eyeglasses) instructs members of New York's Actors Studio, which was founded in 1947 by Elia Kazan, Cheryl Crawford, and Robert Lewis. Strasberg, who joined the studio in 1948, taught a modified form of Stanislavsky's Method to such members as Paul Newman, Marlon Brando, James Dean, and Marilyn Monroe (seen here at left).

streets of New York, he would study the passersby, imprinting on his memory their features and distinctive movements. "He would take . . . their voices, their expressions, their gestures, and it would become part of him without his having to work on it," remembered Dizzy Sheridan. "I don't think he did it so much as it overtook him because he was so impressionable."

The Method had a strong influence on Dean's work as an actor. As time passed, however, he began to lose interest in the sessions held at the Studio. Apparently, he did not take criticism well, and he was too much of an individual to submit to Strasberg's methods. According to Elia Kazan, "Dean was scarcely at the Studio at all. He came in only a few times. I remember him sitting in the front row, a surly mess. He never participated in anything."

Strasberg, on the other hand, believed that it was a deep-set wariness that kept Dean away from the Studio: "He was sensitive about letting people in too close. He seemed to shy away from people. He was afraid they would get to know him."

It was during this period, nonetheless, that Dean attached himself to a 16-year-old actress named Barbara Glenn. Neurotic, talented, and good-looking, she shared many characteristics with Dean. They were instantly attracted to each other, and within a matter of weeks they had fallen in love. Unfortunately, their frequent quarrels caused them both a great deal of pain and eventually tore them apart. "Jimmy was a terribly destructive person," said Glenn. "Our relationship was destructive."

In the beginning, however, there were good times for both. With his earnings from *Jaguar,* Dean bought a used motorcycle, and with Glenn seated nervously behind him, they would zip up and down the busy streets of New York. One of their favorite spots was Greenwich Village, known for its casual, bohemian atmosphere. Glenn enjoyed the hours she spent with Dean, but she hated and feared his motorcycle. She was convinced that sooner or later it would lead to tragedy.

"I remember half my life with Jimmy was waiting for him because he was always late," she said, "and I was always wondering if he was going to make it. There was an inevitability about Jimmy's death from the day I met him, which frightened me because I always had the feeling that somehow, someway, someday he's not going to show up."

5 New York: Act Two

In 1953, with the help of his agent, James Dean began to build up an impressive list of television credits. He appeared on 17 programs and had the opportunity to work with a number of veteran stars, including Mary Astor, Dorothy Gish, Ronald Reagan, Hume Cronyn, and Jessica Tandy.

Television in the early 1950s was an exciting and experimental medium, but it had its drawbacks. No one pretended that it could compete with the professionalism of Hollywood. Actress Gloria Swanson, who was one of the first stars to get her own TV show, admitted that most programming in the early days "looked cheap and thrown-together . . . too black-and-white, too crude."

Nevertheless, Dean enjoyed his television work. Each new assignment gave him an opportunity to become a different character, and he was able to make use of the techniques he had learned at the Actors Studio. Most of his early television appearances consisted of walk-on parts, with little dialogue. It was not until November 1953 that he was given his first starring role in "A Long Time Till Dawn," a Kraft Television Theater drama written by Rod Serling.

Dean enjoyed his television work, and was able to make use of the techniques he had learned at the Actors Studio. According to one producer, Dean "could be alternately jolly, charming and funny, then 20 minutes later off by himself 'sulking.' But he only *appeared* to be sulking—he was actually inside of himself."

Dean's character, according to Serling, "was a terribly upset, psyched-out kid, a precursor to the hooked generation of the sixties."

Serling realized when he wrote the teleplay that he was creating a new type of screen character, one exactly suited to Dean's talents. Before World War II, American teenagers were usually portrayed in a cheerful, positive way. Even juvenile delinquents were often revealed to be basically good kids. The postwar years, however, witnessed a change in America's social mores. Young people began to question authority, to lose confidence in their elders, and to challenge long-standing ideas concerning morality and "acceptable" behavior. According to Dean's girlfriend, Barbara Glenn, young people after the war "were not sure what they really wanted, what life was about. People were . . . well, they were lost. They had no goals."

Hollywood continued to insist that teenagers were as upbeat as ever, but the young writers working for television knew better. They, too, were having doubts about society and were anxious to create characters who could accurately reflect those doubts. "We could portray it immediately too," said Serling, "write a script one week and have it on the air the next."

In "A Long Time Till Dawn," Dean played a deeply troubled youth given to fits of violence. Serling called his performance brilliant: "I can't imagine anyone playing that particular role better. I think this was his first big role in television and his behavior was very restrained and uncomfortable, but even then there was an excitement and intensity about him that he transmitted viscerally to the television audience."

Dean had other good parts, as well. In "Death Is My Neighbor," a drama for CBS, he played a psychotic janitor cut down in a hail of police gunfire. Famed Shakespearean actor Walter Hampden was the featured star, but according to *Variety,* it was Dean who stole the show, delivering "a magnetic performance that brought a routine [melodrama] alive." *Variety* went on to compare Dean to Marlon Brando, who had become a Broadway star in 1947 in Tennessee Williams's searing play, *A Streetcar Named Desire. Variety* noted that Dean's character was similar to that of Brando's, "but he gave his role the individuality and nuances . . . which it required. He's got quite a future ahead of him."

As Dean's television appearances became more frequent, he attracted the attention of female fans, who began to write to him. Dean told a friend that he was constantly receiving letters "from old ladies watching television. They tell me about how they want me to wear tighter pants. They have this televison club of ladies from 50 to 75 and they sit there checking the cats out. . . . It's really hard to believe."

Marlon Brando, Jessica Tandy, and Kim Hunter perform in Tennessee Williams's *A Streetcar Named Desire.* Brando may have admired Dean as an actor, but he disliked him as a person. "[Dean] was always trying to get close to me," Brando told writer Truman Capote. "He used to call up asking for me and I'd listen on my answering service but I never spoke to him."

By the end of 1953, Dean had established himself as one of the most promising young actors on television. He had also acquired a reputation for being difficult to work with. On the set, Dean was often moody and disrespectful. He was frequently late for rehearsal and, to the frustration of his costars, he tended to mumble his lines.

"Live television was a very precise business," remembered Mary Astor, "with word cues for camera cuts. Timing had to be accurate in word and action—or you could find yourself off the air or with time left over." In 1955, she and Dean appeared together in "The Thief," a televised drama for ABC. At the final dress rehearsal, she said, "Jimmy was six feet away from me in one scene and I could barely hear what he was saying, and what I could hear seemed to have very little to do with the script."

On the air, Dean's performances were outstanding, even brilliant, but he had a habit of exasperating his directors beforehand by asking detailed questions about his character. Sometimes, these questions were genuinely helpful to the cast; on other occasions, they served only to irritate and demoralize the crew. Behind Dean's back, people joked about his reliance on the Method, but Dean felt he could not give a believable performance unless he could relate it to some aspect of his life.

At the Actors Studio, Lee Strasberg would ask, "What do you mean to *accomplish* in this scene?" It was a valid question, and Dean tried to answer it whenever he rehearsed. Often, this meant that he would play a scene differently each time. According to one producer, "Jimmy was always thinking about his character, and every time he did he would discover new things about him that he'd want to say." Naturally, this upset his co-workers, who never quite knew what to expect when the cameras started to roll.

"He would do anything you wanted him to do," said director Don Medford, "but he would never be able to repeat the same moment, and that, unfortunately, in-cluded the staging. In other words he was the antithesis of being mechanical."

By mid-1953, Bill Bast had returned to California and Dean was living by himself in a top-floor apartment on West Sixty-eighth Street. It was an extremely small space, but Dean seemed to like it. Dusty sunlight streamed through a porthole window, revealing a colorful assort-ment of beloved objects: pen-and-ink drawings, a flute, a used Leica camera, a pair of bongo drums, a blood-stained matador's cape hanging on the wall, a hot plate, Billie Holiday recordings, and a plant growing in a coffee can.

And, of course, books—piles and piles of books. Dean believed that it was his responsibility as an actor to explore all fields of knowledge. "In the short span of his lifetime an actor must learn all there is to know," he once said, "experience all there is to experience—or approach that state as closely as possible. He must be superhuman in his endless struggle to inform himself."

In December 1953, Jane Deacy encouraged Dean to audition for a role in a new play called *The Immoralist.* Adapted from a short novel by French author André Gide, it told the story of an alcoholic woman named Marcelline, who discovers on her honeymoon that her husband, Michel, has homosexual tendencies. Dean was intrigued by the role of Bachir, a conniving, homosexual houseboy who brings Michel to an awareness of his sexual identity. Dean sensed that the part was rich with possi-bilities and, if played correctly, might be the big break he was waiting for.

When he showed up at the Ziegfeld Theater to audi-tion, he was wearing a strange mishmash of clothing: ill-fitting cowboy boots, ragged blue jeans, a Russian fur hat, and a moth-eaten vest and coat. As soon as he began to read, however, everyone forgot about his peculiar

appearance. He instantly slipped into the character of Bachir, capturing the unscrupulousness and sexual menace that the role required. "It was obvious to all of us that he was great," said Ruth Goetz, who had written the play with her husband, Augustus. Dean was immediately given the part.

When he told Barbara Glenn the good news, she was delighted. "But I knew that Jimmy was scared," she recalled. "He was always scared. That's why he had such an 'I don't give a damn' facade, to cover the fear, but it was an artist's fear of 'Can I do it?' It was joy and fear mixed together."

To prepare for the role of Bachir, Dean interviewed a number of his homosexual friends. He also spent a great deal of time rehearsing his movements. He wanted to appear seductive onstage, but not effeminate. In one of the most interesting scenes in *The Immoralist,* Bachir performs a sensuous dance for Michel. Dressed in a loose-fitting caftan, his arms lifted gracefully in the air, Dean snipped a small pair of scissors in time to the music. The dance, said one observer, "was very slow and very deliberate, and very *man to man.*"

At rehearsals for the play, Dean lived up to his reputation as a troublesome actor. According to Ruth Goetz, he refused to memorize the script, ignored the people in charge, and would not take his work seriously: "[The director] would say something to him and he would make a point of not doing it. He drove us up the wall." Later, Goetz called Dean the most exasperating young actor she had ever worked with.

Despite its dramatic potential, *The Immoralist* was a play beset by problems. The script was continually being revised, the director was replaced midstream, and much to Dean's disappointment, the size of his role was steadily reduced. The new director, Daniel Mann, was convinced that Dean was deliberately defying him and this caused

Opposite:
Dean performs a sensuous dance as Bachir in André Gide's *The Immoralist.* Before the Broadway play opened, Dean told a friend, "I don't want to be a good actor. I want to be the best actor there is."

Initially, director Elia Kazan thought he wanted Marlon Brando to play the role of Cal Trask, but the more he contemplated it, he knew that Dean was perfect for the part.

tempers to flare. On one occasion, Mann chased Dean down the street, threatening to kill him.

In early January, *The Immoralist* moved to Philadelphia for its out-of-town tryout. Dean's acting on opening night was strong, but his subsequent performances were maddeningly uneven. He was quickly losing interest in his work and at one point considered dropping out of the play. In a letter to Barbara Glenn, he complained that it was "the most boring dull cast and show I have ever seen."

During the three-week Philadelphia run, a Hollywood writer named Paul Osborn happened to see the show. He liked Dean's performance and, the next day, he called his boss, Elia Kazan, urging him to see *The Immoralist* when it came to New York. There was a young actor in the cast, Osborn said, whom he might want to check out. His name was James Dean.

Kazan, who was considered one of Hollywood's top directors, remembered Dean's work at the Actors Studio. Personally, he disliked Dean's rebellious streak, but he realized that he might be able to turn it to his advantage. Kazan was then in the process of casting his next movie, *East of Eden,* and was having trouble finding an actor to play the role of Cal Trask, a moody adolescent. He thought he wanted Marlon Brando, but the more he considered it, he thought Dean might be an even better choice.

Kazan was one of the few directors in Hollywood who preferred to work with unknown actors. They gave better performances, he maintained: "They're like fighters on their way up. It's a life or death struggle for them and they give their utmost to the role." To please Paul Osborn, and to see how Dean was progressing as an actor, Kazan promised to see the show.

After a week of previews, *The Immoralist* opened in New York at the Royale Theater on February 8, 1954. It happened to be Dean's 23rd birthday, and his performance that night was superb. Marcus and Ortense Winslow flew in from Fairmount for the occasion and were thrilled to witness their nephew's triumph on the Broadway stage. *The Immoralist* was dismissed by most critics as a dull production, but Dean received excellent reviews and, several months later, he won a Daniel Blum Theater World Award as one of the most promising personalities of the year.

In light of his success in the play, Dean's actions on opening night might seem deliberately self-destructive. While taking his curtain call, Dean lifted the folds of his caftan and curtsied to the audience. Everyone laughed and gave him a big round of applause. Backstage, however, Daniel Mann was furious. In front of the entire cast, he threatened to fire Dean if he ever pulled a stunt like that again. Instead of apologizing, Dean handed the director his two weeks' notice. He was quitting the play.

Dean's decision was not as spontaneous as it appeared. As he saw it, *The Immoralist* had served its purpose. It had brought him to the attention of the New York critics and that was what he had been waiting for. In any case, he had no faith in the play, nor did he wish to run the risk of being typecast in homosexual roles. Dean wanted out, and he used Mann's opening-night tongue-lashing as the perfect excuse to quit.

He stayed with the play for two more weeks, giving his final performance on February 23. By then, Elia Kazan had seen the show and he asked Dean to come to his office at Warner Brothers for an interview.

Dean showed up, but his sloppy clothing and surly attitude irritated Kazan, who remembered the meeting vividly: "I didn't like the expression on [Dean's] face, so I kept him waiting. I also wanted to see how he'd react to that. It seemed that I'd outtoughed him, because when I called him into my office, he'd dropped the belligerent pose. We tried to talk, but conversation was not his gift, so we sat looking at each other."

Just when Kazan thought it was a lost cause, Dean surprised him by asking if he wanted to go for a ride on his motorcycle. Kazan agreed, thinking it might be a good way to break the ice. It was a decision he quickly regretted. Gunning his motor, Dean tore down the street, weaving in and out of busy traffic, deliberately trying to scare the director. Kazan was a nervous wreck by the time he got back to the office, but he was also tremendously excited. He knew instinctively that Dean was perfect for the part of Cal Trask.

That afternoon, he called Paul Osborn to share the news. He also made arrangements for Dean to be photographed with Julie Harris, a brilliant, 29-year-old actress whom he was about to sign for the female lead. Finally, he sent Dean to meet novelist John Steinbeck, the author of *East of Eden*. "John thought Dean a snotty kid," said Kazan. "I said that was irrelevant; wasn't he Cal? John said he sure as hell was, and that was it."

Shortly thereafter, Dean made a screen test with actor Paul Newman. Both men performed well, but Dean seemed more believable as an 18-year-old. He also had a dark, troubled side that was appropriate for the character. Kazan knew that the success of *East of Eden* would depend largely on the actor he chose to play Cal. More than $1.5 million would be spent on the picture, and he could not afford to make a mistake.

"There was no point in attempting to cast it better or nicer," Kazan said later. "Jimmy was it."

COSTUME DEPT. PROD. 810
NAME JAMES DEAN
PART CAL TRASK
CHG.# 2   SC. 51-66
EXT. RAIL ROAD YARDS

6 ★ East of Eden

Accompanied by Elia Kazan, James Dean flew to California on March 8, 1954. It was Dean's first time in an airplane, and he thoroughly enjoyed the nine-hour flight. Upon arriving in Los Angeles, he asked Kazan if they could stop briefly at the Sawtelle Veterans Administration Hospital, where his father worked. Kazan agreed, thinking it might be interesting to watch the two interact.

Dean went inside the hospital, emerging a few minutes later with Winton at his side. Kazan immediately picked up on the tension between them. Winton, wearing glasses and a white lab coat, looked distinctly uncomfortable. After introducing Kazan, Dean tried to make conversation, but it was painfully clear he had nothing to say. It was almost as though he and his father were strangers. At last, Winton said good-bye and Dean climbed back into the limousine, visibly shaken by the encounter.

From there he and Kazan drove to the Warner Brothers Studio in Burbank, where *East of Eden* was scheduled to begin shooting in two months. In the meantime, Dean had no place to stay—certainly, he had no desire to live with

---

Dean is seen here on location in Salinas for *East of Eden*. "Jimmy wasn't easy to work with because it was all new to him," said director Elia Kazan. "He was like an animal might be. Fretful, uncertain."

71

his father and stepmother. Casually, Kazan suggested that he share a room with Dick Davalos, the actor who would be playing his brother, Aron, in the film. Sibling rivalry was an important theme in the picture, and Kazan wanted Dean and Davalos to get to know each other before filming began. Crucially, he wanted to build up an emotional tension between the two men. By forcing them to live together in a one-room apartment, Kazan was hoping to generate plenty of friction between them.

The ruse worked. Within days, the two actors were not only fighting, but had developed a close and disturbing relationship that mirrored the complex bond between Cal and Aron Trask. "It was a mind blower, truly," remembered Davalos. "We were so into those roles, me and Jimmy. . . . It took me two years to get over that part."

East of Eden had been published two years earlier, in 1952. Considered one of John Steinbeck's less successful works, it tells the story of a pious man, Adam Trask, his destructive wife, Kate, and their twin sons, Aron and Cal. Steinbeck implies that the boys were fathered by two different men—this, supposedly, would account for Aron's "good" nature and Cal's "wicked" nature. Soon after giving birth, Kate decides to leave Adam, who raises the boys with the belief that their mother is dead. When Cal is a teenager, however, he learns that Kate is operating a brothel in a nearby town. He uses this perverse knowledge to emotionally destroy his brother, Aron; this, in turn, causes Adam to suffer a severe stroke.

Because it would be unwieldy to depict the lengthy Trask story in its entirety, Kazan decided to film only a small portion of Steinbeck's novel. Wisely, he chose to concentrate not on Kate, but on the more interesting (and more realistic) character of Cal, a rebellious youth who believes that he is evil. In this respect, Kazan's casting was superb, because James Dean believed that he, too, was born wicked. Why else, he often asked his friends,

had his parents abandoned him? Kazan instantly recognized the similarities between the script and Dean's life, and, to some extent, this dictated his decision to hire Dean for the part.

In early April, Dean signed a contract with Warner Brothers guaranteeing him a weekly salary of $1,000. Kazan then sent him north to the agricultural town of Salinas, where portions of *Eden* would be shot. The director envisioned Cal as a healthy, well-fed farm boy, and at the moment Dean looked thin and pale, a creature of the city. To remedy this, Kazan told him to sit in the sun and to drink a pint of cream a day. He also instructed Dean to get plenty of sleep. As Kazan remarked to his assistant director, "You'd need two-by-fours to prop up the bags under his eyes."

James Dean, Dick Davalos, and Julie Harris appear in a scene from *East of Eden*. According to Elia Kazan, Harris "was goodness itself with Dean, kind and patient and everlastingly sympathetic. She would adjust her performance to whatever the new kid did."

73

Dean spent the rest of the month in Salinas, John Steinbeck's hometown. In addition to visiting some of the locales that would appear in the film, he learned how to ride a horse and spent time talking with the lettuce and artichoke farmers about their crops. He also picked up a reasonably good Salinas accent.

Though Dean had plenty to keep him occupied, he felt himself gradually sinking into despair. He was worried about his upcoming performance and, as the weeks passed, he allowed his thoughts to darken. "I don't like it here [in Salinas]," he wrote to Barbara Glenn on April 26. "I don't like people here. I like it home (N.Y.) and I like you and I want to see you. Must I always be miserable? I try so hard to make people reject me. Why? . . . I WANT TO DIE. . . . Write me please. I'm sad most of the time. Awful lonely too." He signed the letter "Jim (Brando Clift) Dean," invoking the names of his two favorite actors, Marlon Brando and Montgomery Clift, both of whom belonged to the Actors Studio.

Shortly after returning to Los Angeles, Dean wrote another letter to Glenn, this time relaying good news: "I haven't written because I have fallen in love. It had to happen sooner or later. It's not a very good picture of him but that's 'Cisco the Kid' the new member of the family. He gives me confidence. He makes my hands and my heart strong."

Cisco was a two-year-old palomino, which Dean had purchased for $250. To his delight, he was allowed to keep the horse on the studio lot, but the arrangement proved far from ideal. According to Kazan, Dean kept wandering off "to feed or curry or just look at his gorgeous animal. I finally had the horse exiled to a farm in the San Fernando Valley. Then Jimmy bought a motorbike, but I stopped that too. I told him I didn't want to chance an accident, and that he absolutely couldn't ride the bike until the film was over."

Opposite:
In one of *East of Eden*'s **most dramatic scenes, Cal (James Dean) confronts his father, Adam Trask (Raymond Massey). A dignified and respected actor, Massey hated working with the 23-year-old Dean. "You never know what he's going to say or do," he told Elia Kazan, echoing the complaints of many of Dean's co-workers.**

Not about to be deprived of wheels, Dean defiantly purchased a flashy red MG sports car. That same evening, he took his costar, Julie Harris, for a daredevil ride in the Hollywood hills. She remembered it as one of the most frightening experiences of her life. Convinced she was about to fall out of the convertible, she wanted to cry out, to tell Dean to slow down, but she knew that any sign of cowardice would only make him drive faster. "He was testing me," she said, "to see if I'd take everything he had to give."

By mid-May, Kazan had assembled most of the cast for *East of Eden*. In addition to Dean, Harris, and Dick Davalos, he had hired Raymond Massey and Jo Van Fleet to play Adam and Kate Trask. Massey, a respected and dignified actor, took an instant dislike to Dean, whom he regarded as crude and unprofessional. Dean was well aware of Massey's disapproval and during rehearsals a lively animosity developed between them. At one point, Massey, in a rage, threatened to walk off the set, but Kazan pleaded with him to be patient. "Bear with me, Ray," he said, "I'm getting solid gold."

Shooting on the picture began on May 27 in Mendocino, a lovely area north of San Francisco. A week later, the cast and crew moved south to Salinas to capture some of the locations Steinbeck had described in his book. By mid-June, everyone was back in Burbank to film the interior scenes. At first, Dean was worried about his acting, but Kazan was extremely pleased with what he saw in the screening room. As he had hoped, Dean's portrayal of Cal Trask was at once explosive, tender, sensuous, and tormented. It was, by any standard, a film debut of astonishing breadth.

East of Eden is full of memorable sequences, but one in particular stands out. Near the end of the film, Cal arranges a surprise birthday party for his father, Adam. Full of emotion, he hands his father a small wrapped

Opposite:
Director Elia Kazan and actors Marlon Brando, Julie Harris, and James Dean meet on the set of *East of Eden*. After the film's release, Brando was heard to denigrate Dean's performance: "The kid is wearing my last year's clothes and using my last year's talent."

package. At that moment, his brother, Aron, steals the limelight by announcing his engagement to his girlfriend, Abra, a spontaneous "gift" that pleases the old man enormously.

Adam then tears open Cal's package, revealing a large sum of money that Cal has secretly earned by raising and selling beans. Instead of expressing gratitude, Adam rejects the gift, which he angrily denounces as a heartless example of wartime profiteering. He takes this opportunity to remind Cal what a disappointment he has been as a son: "If you want to give me a present, give me a good life. That would be something I could value."

In the original script, Cal was supposed to give a loud scream and run from the room. Dean must have sensed, however, that this would not be a satisfying response. As a Method actor, he remembered how awful it felt to be rejected by his own father and, as the cameras continued to roll, he decided to go with his instincts, to release all the anger and frustration he felt toward Winton Dean. Letting the wad of money flutter to the floor, he fell against Raymond Massey, desperately clinging to him, emitting pained animal noises. Massey was deeply shocked and tried to pull away, which only intensified the drama. The scene, as captured by Kazan, is brilliantly performed, almost unbearable to watch in its emotional power.

"At the very end of the shooting, the last few days," remembered Kazan, "you felt that a star was going to be born." Hollywood insiders, meanwhile, were buzzing with the news of Kazan's latest discovery, and one day Marlon Brando visited the set, curious to meet the young man who was causing such a sensation. According to Kazan, Dean idolized Brando: "Everyone knew that, because he dropped his voice to a cathedral hush when he talked about Marlon. . . . [Brando] was very gracious to Jimmy, who was so adoring that he seemed shrunken and twisted in misery." Brando apparently admired Dean as an actor, but, to the latter's disappointment, Brando never indicated any desire to strike up a friendship.

During the filming of *East of Eden,* Dean purchased an expensive camera, and when he had some free time he would explore the soundstages, taking pictures. One afternoon, he watched Judy Garland perform a dance routine for her "comeback" film, *A Star Is Born.* Another day, he wandered down the street to the soundstage where Victor Saville was directing *The Silver Chalice,* a biblical tale of epic proportions. Today, *The Silver Chalice* is regarded as one of Hollywood's silliest productions, but at the time it was considered an important and prestigious project. In addition to giving Paul Newman his first screen role, it featured a 22-year-old actress named Pier Angeli, who would soon become Dean's lover.

Born on the island of Sardinia in 1932, Anna Maria Pierangeli was a beautiful child. "She had the face of a Madonna," said one journalist, "pure and full of grace." After appearing in two Italian films, she came to America, accompanied by her widowed mother and her two sisters. By the time she met Dean, she was considered one of Hollywood's most promising starlets (as well as one of the town's most stylish dressers).

Within a very short time, she and Dean had fallen in love. They visited each other on the set and were seen holding hands in the studio commissary. Years later, in a misty-eyed interview, Pier called their romance a beautiful thing, full of innocence and quiet understanding: "We were like Romeo and Juliet, together and inseparable. Sometimes on the beach we loved each other so much we just wanted to walk together into the sea holding hands because we knew then that we would always be together."

As *Eden* neared completion, Dean's name began to appear with greater frequency in the trade papers.

Everyone at Warner Brothers was raving about his performance. He was the next Marlon Brando, the executives predicted. To capitalize on this good word of mouth, the publicity department arranged for Dean to lunch with Hedda Hopper, Hollywood's most powerful gossip columnist. Hopper had heard good things about Warner's "boy genius," and she was looking forward to interviewing him in the studio commissary. Their "luncheon," however, was a disaster from start to finish, and in her widely read column, Hopper painted a devastating portrait of a sulky and immature "star" deliberately trying to shock the press.

"The latest genius sauntered in," she wrote, "dressed like a bum, and slouched down in silence at a table away from mine. He hooked another chair with his toe, dragged it close enough to put his feet up, while he watched me from the corner of his eye. Then he stood up to inspect the framed photographs of Warner stars that covered the wall by his head. He chose one of them, spat in its eye, wiped off his spittle with a handkerchief, then like a ravenous hyena, started to gulp the food that had been served him." A Warner press agent offered to introduce Hopper to Dean, but the columnist refused. She had seen enough. "If this is the kind of talent they're importing," she later wrote, "they can send it right back, as far as I'm concerned."

East of Eden finished shooting on August 13, 1954. By then, Dean and Pier Angeli were thinking about getting married. To a fan magazine reporter, Dean explained why he found Pier so attractive. "[She] is a rare person," he said. "Unlike most Hollywood girls, she is real and genuine. Her only trouble is that she gets confused by listening to too many advisors."

Pier's main adviser was her mother, who strongly disapproved of the relationship. Dean was sloppy and rude, she said, and—worst of all—he was not a Catholic.

Opposite:
Dean focuses a camera on his Italian girlfriend, actress Pier Angeli. Dean fell madly in love with Pier and asked her to marry him. Pier's strict mother, however, found Dean an unsuitable match for the beautiful and promising starlet.

To please Pier's mother, Dean agreed to be baptized, but Mrs. Pierangeli could not be swayed. She was certain her beautiful daughter could find a more suitable husband than scruffy James Dean.

Then, suddenly, the situation became more complicated. According to one of Dean's biographers, Pier told Dean that she thought she was pregnant. The timing was awkward: Within days, Dean was scheduled to fly to New York to appear on two television programs. He asked Pier to go with him to New York, where they could be married, but she refused. An elopement, she said, would break her mother's heart. Angry words were exchanged between them and, in a foul mood, Dean left for the East Coast. He was unwilling to end the relationship, however, and whenever he had a few moments to spare, he would call Pier long-distance, begging her to reconsider.

While Dean was in New York, Pier went out with Vic Damone, a popular singer whom she had dated a few years earlier. The sparks between them were rekindled and, to the astonishment of many in Hollywood, Pier announced to the press that she and Damone were engaged to be married. When Dean heard the news, he was shocked. He tried repeatedly to telephone Pier, but she refused to accept his calls. For days he felt frustrated and upset, barely able to concentrate on his work.

Had he been able to see the situation clearly, Dean would have realized that Pier had no choice but to get married as quickly as possible. Her pregnancy would soon become apparent, and in 1954 it would have been unthinkable for a young starlet to have a baby out of wedlock. A month later, on November 23, Pier married Vic Damone at St. Timothy's in Hollywood. More than 600 guests attended the ceremony, but Dean was not among them. Pier had specifically asked him to stay away.

On August 21, 1955, Pier Angeli gave birth to an 8-pound, 13-ounce son, whom she named Perry. It is tempting to assume that Dean fathered the baby, though it could very well have been Damone's. In any event, Pier's shotgun marriage ended in divorce, and years later, speaking to an interviewer, she reminisced about her relationship with James Dean. He was the only man she had ever loved, she said, and she wished she had married him when she had the chance. A second marriage to musician Armando Trotajoli also ended in divorce. Pier Angeli was attempting a professional comeback when she died of a drug overdose in 1971. She was 39 years old.

7 ★ Rebel Without a Cause

In January 1955, two months after James Dean had returned from New York, Elia Kazan arranged for *East of Eden* to be shown to a preview audience in the Los Angeles area. The hysteria that accompanied the event took the director completely by surprise. "The instant [Dean] appeared on the screen," he recalled, "hundreds of girls began to scream. They'd been waiting for him, it seemed—how come or why, I don't know. The response of the balcony reminded me of . . . Niagara Falls spilling over."

Subsequent previews were equally successful, and the word quickly spread through Hollywood that James Dean was a brilliant actor. This annoyed columnist Hedda Hopper, who shivered at the memory of her distasteful luncheon with Dean in the Warner Brothers commissary. Nevertheless, as a journalist, she felt it was her duty to keep abreast of the newest film stars. Reluctantly, she telephoned Kazan, who arranged for a private screening.

Hopper was fully prepared to dislike Dean's performance; instead, she was profoundly moved by what she saw. "In the projection room I sat spellbound," she later wrote. "I couldn't remember ever having seen a young man

---

In *Rebel Without a Cause,* Dean plays Jim Stark, a troubled 17-year-old who tries, unsuccessfully, to fit in with the other students at Dawson High School. "I've never met anyone with the ability of Dean," said director Nick Ray. "I'm sure he'll bring performances to the screen the likes of which haven't yet been thought of."

Hollywood actress and journalist Hedda Hopper was profoundly moved by Dean's performance in *East of Eden*. She later wrote, "I couldn't remember ever having seen a young man with such power, so many facets of expression, so much sheer invention as this actor."

with such power, so many facets of expression, so much sheer invention as this actor."

Hopper immediately contacted Jack Warner, the head of the studio, requesting a formal interview with Dean. "He may not want to [cooperate] with me after what I wrote," she admitted. "If he doesn't, I shan't hold it against him." A few days later, Dean showed up on Hopper's doorstep, wearing black pants and a black leather jacket. Gently, the columnist scolded him for his outrageous behavior in the commissary. Dean admitted that he had been testing her: "I wanted to see if anybody in this town had guts enough to tell the truth." From that moment on, Hedda Hopper became one of Dean's strongest allies in Hollywood.

On March 9, 1955, *East of Eden* received its world premiere at the Astor Theater in New York. A benefit for the Actors Studio, it was a splashy, star-studded affair, but Dean deliberately chose to absent himself. "I'm sorry," he told Jane Deacy, "but I can't handle that scene." The glare of publicity made him feel uneasy.

The reviews of *East of Eden* were largely favorable. "[It] has the look of truth," said the *New York Herald-Tribune.* "It also has a wistful beauty and a great deal of power." *Time* magazine was even more complimentary: "The picture is brilliant entertainment and more than that, it announces a new star, James Dean, whose prospects look as bright as any young actor's since Marlon Brando. . . . Dean, a young man from Indiana, is unquestionably the biggest news Hollywood has made in 1955."

Although most critics agreed that Dean's acting was superb, there were a few, like Bosley Crowther of the *New York Times,* who were unimpressed. Crowther, in fact, was appalled by much of Dean's performance: "He scuffs his feet. . . he pouts, he sputters, he leans against walls, he rolls his eyes, he swallows his words, he ambles slack-kneed—all like Marlon Brando used to do. Never have we seen a performer so clearly follow another's style. Mr. Kazan should be spanked for permitting him to do such a sophomoric thing. Whatever there might be of reasonable torment in this youngster is buried beneath the clumsy display."

Crowther was not the only critic to point out a resemblance between Dean and Brando, but in retrospect it seems irrelevant to compare them. "They're two totally different kinds of personalities," said Lee Strasberg, who had worked with both men at the Actors Studio. "What was common at that time was the *characters* they played . . . what we call today the anti-hero, the person who cannot express himself, the person who is not a hero in the ordinary sense of the word." Strasberg's observation was correct, but the comparisons to Brando would continue to haunt Dean nevertheless.

Two weeks after the premiere of *East of Eden,* Dean started work on his second film for Warner Brothers, *Rebel Without a Cause.* Loosely based on a book by Robert Lindner, it chronicles 24 hours in the life of Jim Stark, a troubled 17-year-old who has just moved to a new town. Near the start of the picture, he tries to make friends with Judy, the girl next door, but she gives him the cold shoulder. His trouble continues at Dawson High School, where he is immediately rejected as an outsider.

To complicate the situation, Jim has an anguished relationship with his overbearing mother and henpecked father, who fail to understand their son's torment. By clinging stubbornly to their old-fashioned notions of "correct" behavior, they inadvertently push Jim to the edge of disaster.

Rebel Without a Cause was directed by Nicholas Ray, who was anxious to make a film about juvenile delinquency, which in 1955 was becoming a widespread problem in America. To ensure that the screenplay was accurate, Ray sought the advice of psychiatrists, police officers, and social workers. He also interviewed a number of teenage delinquents in the Los Angeles area.

"In listening to these adolescents talk about their lives and their acts," he said, "two impressions always recurred. What they did had a terrifying, morose aimlessness—like the 16-year-old boy who ran his car into a group of young children 'just for fun'—and a feeling of bitter isolation and resentment about their families."

The script for *Rebel* had undergone numerous revisions by the time Dean was hired, but Ray never lost sight of his ultimate goal. He wanted to portray, in the course of a single day, a young man's difficult transition from adolescence to adulthood. "The purpose of the film," said screenwriter Stewart Stern, "was to tell the story of a generation growing up—in one night."

Before shooting on *Rebel* began, Dean sold his red MG and purchased a white Porsche Speedster for $4,000. On the weekend of March 26 and 27, he entered the eighth annual Palm Springs Road Races. The other drivers did not take him seriously, assuming it was some kind of publicity stunt. Dean surprised everyone by finishing first in the amateur class and second in the professional class. Considering his lack of technique, it was an unexpected victory, one that gave him a great deal of personal pleasure.

"I encouraged the racing," admitted Nick Ray. "It was good for Jimmy to do something on his own with clarity and precision."

Ray, meanwhile, was assembling the cast for *Rebel Without a Cause*. To play Jim Stark's parents, he hired Jim Backus and Ann Doran. (Backus, known primarily as a comedian, later starred in the popular TV series "Gilligan's Island.") Ray also hired a 16-year-old actress named Natalie Wood to play the role of Judy, who snubs Jim on her way to school. Later, after her boyfriend is killed in a tragic accident, Judy falls in love with Jim. Together they hide out in a deserted mansion near Griffith Planetarium, where the film reaches its violent climax.

A Hollywood veteran, Wood had worked with Dean a few months earlier in a teleplay for CBS. Ray admired her work, but he had doubts about casting her in *Rebel*—he did not believe that audiences would accept her as a juvenile delinquent. Wood fought hard for the part, however, and once in front of the camera, she delivered an outstanding performance.

Rebel Without a Cause began shooting in Burbank on March 28, 1955. In his attempt to give it authenticity,

Natalie Wood and James Dean first met while filming "I'm a Fool," a teleplay for CBS that was broadcast in November 1954. By the time shooting on *Rebel* began, the two actors had become close friends.

Ray told his largely teenage cast that he was open to suggestions for enhancing the film. They should feel free, he said, to improvise their dialogue and experiment with their characterizations.

"He wanted the movie to come from us, rather than from his direction," said Steffi Skolsky, who played one of the gang members at Dawson High. "[During rehearsals] Nick told us we were playing individually instead of together. So we all went out together, except for Jimmy. We went to the beach, and climbed around a deserted warehouse one night, to get the feeling of being a group. By the time we were ready to start shooting, we were really thinking as one."

The film opens with a shot of Jim Stark, dressed in a suit, lying on the sidewalk, drunk. He is holding a windup toy monkey, which he gently covers with a piece of paper. The gesture, improvised by Dean on the spot, is both paternal and childlike, capturing the strange duality that was an important part of his screen persona. "In that . . . bit," observed one writer, "Jimmy involved the audience in the character he was playing: an isolated and defenseless teenager in a world of his own creation."

A moment later, a patrol car pulls up, and Jim is taken to the police station, where he is searched. Instead of resisting—which would have been a conventional response—Dean began to giggle. Obviously, the frisking tickled. Again, it was a clever improvisation that surprised everyone, including Dennis Hopper, who played one of the gang members. "Where did that [giggle] come from?" he later wondered. "It came from genius, that's where it came from. And that was all him. Nobody directed him to do that. James Dean directed James Dean."

In Ray's determination to make the film look realistic, the violence sometimes got out of hand. Real switchblades, for instance, were used during a fight sequence at the planetarium. During one take, Dean was accidentally cut by his opponent. Ray noticed blood on his neck and immediately yelled "Cut!" Dean, who had gone to great lengths to work himself into the proper emotional state, was furious at Ray for stopping the camera. "Can't you see this is a real moment?" he yelled at the director. "Don't you ever cut a scene while I'm having a real moment. That's what I'm here for!"

Some of the most agonizing scenes in the picture portray Jim's frustrating relationship with his father, a man who means well but is unable to provide the kind of guidance Jim so desperately needs. Jim Backus had met Dean a few months earlier at a mutual friend's house. On the set of *Rebel,* Backus was deeply impressed by the single-minded passion with which Dean approached his art.

"He had the greatest power of concentration I have ever encountered," recalled Backus. "He prepared himself so well in advance . . . that the lines were not simply something he had memorized—they were actually a very real part of him. Before the take of any scene, he would go off by himself . . . and think about what he had to do, to the exclusion of everything else. He returned when he felt he was enough in character to shoot the scene."

During the filming of *Rebel,* Dean became extremely interested in the process of moviemaking. Ray later acknowledged that his young star was involved "at every stage in the development of the picture." Dean was fascinated by the nature of Ray's work and began to think that he, too, might like to become a director. He went over the script endlessly, making many suggestions that were incorporated into the movie. According to costar Jim Backus, 24-year-old Dean was "practically the co-director."

Despite the degree of commitment that Dean brought to his work, his behavior on the set was sometimes selfish and unprofessional. On one occasion, for example, he kept the crew waiting for an hour while he listened to classical music in his dressing room. He also had an irritating habit of not acknowledging people when they said hello. "He would look through you as though you didn't exist," said costar Bev Long. Everyone on the set tried to exercise patience, however. They seemed to understand that Dean was a gifted artist whose eccentricities had to be indulged.

In addition to Dean and Natalie Wood, *Rebel* featured a young actor named Sal Mineo, who played the role of Plato, a psychotic weakling who is tormented by the gang at Dawson High. When he wrote the script, Stewart Stern envisioned Plato as a troubled 15-year-old who "wants to find a substitute family for himself . . . and especially a friend who will supply the fatherly protection and warmth he needs."

During the course of the day, Plato and Jim Stark develop a close relationship, one that hints at homosexual undertones. The chemistry between the two actors was unusually potent, and it has been whispered for years that Dean and Mineo had an affair during the making of *Rebel*. There is no evidence, however, to substantiate such a rumor. If anything, Dean appears to have made a conscious effort to suppress his bisexuality in Hollywood. He knew that if this aspect of his private life became a matter of public knowledge, it would probably destroy his career.

As one biographer has observed, however, Dean's bisexuality "seems to be central to who he was and to the fascination he still holds: he's one of the rare stars, like Rock Hudson and Montgomery Clift, who both men and women find sexy."

In *Rebel*, Sal Mineo (left) played the role of Plato, a 15-year-old harassed by the gang at Dawson High. According to Nick Ray, Dean fell in love with Mineo during the making of the picture. "I didn't stop it," said Ray, "because it was helping the film."

Dean leans against his white Porsche Speedster before a March 1955 race in Palm Springs. "Jimmy wanted speed," said racer Ken Miles. "He wanted his body to hurtle across over the ground, the faster the better."

Rebel Without a Cause, which finished shooting in May, was released in late October, one month after Dean's death. Though some critics called it sluggish and melodramatic, it was a box-office success, grossing nearly $5 million. Again, Dean's performance was singled out by the critics, who saw in his portrayal of Jim Stark a maturation of talent.

"Dean projects the wildness, the torment, the crude tenderness of a rootless generation," said *Saturday Review.* "Gone are the Brando mannerisms, gone the too-obvious Kazan touch. He stands out as a remarkable talent; and he was cut down by the same passions he exposes so tellingly in this strange and forceful picture."

By the time he had completed his work on *Rebel,* Dean had entered two more road races. The first was held in Bakersfield, where he finished first in his class. The second event took place in Santa Barbara on Memorial Day weekend. Dean was holding his own in fourth place when engine trouble forced him to quit the track.

Though Dean's skill at the wheel was steadily improving, he had a reckless streak that, had he lived longer, would probably have prevented him from ever becoming a champion racer. "Jimmy was a dreadful driver," remembered screenwriter Irving Shulman. "He would hit a hay bale every time he went around a corner. That's no way to drive, slamming your car around like a billiard ball."

This opinion was seconded by Ken Miles, a racer who had competed against Dean in Palm Springs. According to Miles, Dean "was a menace to himself and other drivers. He wanted to win too much and would take any kind of chance to be first."

Ironically, one of Dean's last appearances on film was a public service announcement for the National Safety Council. Shot on September 17, it featured a short conversation between Dean and actor Gig Young. "People say racing is dangerous," Dean admitted, "but I'd rather take my chances on the track any day than on the highway." Then, twirling a lariat, Dean headed for the door, paused, and turned back to the camera. "And remember," he added, "drive safely—because the life you save may be *mine.*"

8 Giant

In the first week of June 1955, James Dean took the train to Texas to begin work on *Giant,* his third and final picture for Warner Brothers. Budgeted at $5.4 million, *Giant* promised to be a spectacular, all-star production. In addition to Dean, director George Stevens had hired two of the biggest names in Hollywood, Rock Hudson and Elizabeth Taylor. Everyone, especially Stevens, had high hopes for the film. Unfortunately, it would prove to be the most frustrating, and ultimately the most disappointing, experience of Dean's career.

Adapted from a best-selling novel by Edna Ferber, *Giant* told the sprawling story of Bick Benedict (Hudson), a wealthy cattle rancher who marries a beautiful woman named Leslie (Taylor) and brings her back to Reata, his 595,000-acre spread in Texas. Leslie, a Maryland native, is astounded by the vast, open spaces surrounding her, but she is disturbed by her husband's bigotry towards the Mexicans he employs. Soon after her arrival, she sets out to improve living conditions for the underprivileged workers.

Elizabeth Taylor and James Dean, seen here on the set of *Giant,* became close friends during the production of the film. After Dean's death, Taylor went into hysterics and had to be hospitalized for five days.

Another resident on Reata is a surly young ranch hand named Jett Rink (Dean). Upon the accidental death of Bick's sister, Rink inherits 10 acres of the Benedicts' land. He subsequently strikes oil, becomes a multimillionaire, and forms his own corporation, Jettexas. His success angers Benedict, who believes that the economy of Texas should be based on cattle, not oil.

Twenty-five years pass, during which Benedict allows himself to be talked into becoming an oil baron like Rink. At the end of the picture, he manages to overcome his bigotry (and to win Leslie's respect) by standing up for the rights of some Mexicans about to be ejected from a diner. Rink, meanwhile, has turned to alcohol in an attempt to escape his personal unhappiness.

Location shooting began in Virginia, while Dean was still filming *Rebel Without a Cause*. From there the cast and crew moved to the desert town of Marfa, Texas, where the sun beat down mercilessly and fresh water was difficult to obtain. Everyone had to take salt tablets daily to keep from dehydrating.

During the five weeks spent in Marfa, Dean shared a private home with costars Rock Hudson and Chill Wills. Despite their midwestern upbringing, Dean and Hudson had little in common and, as filming progressed, it became clear that neither man liked or trusted the other. Hudson, in particular, felt that Dean was deliberately trying to upstage him in the scenes they shared. Fifteen years later, Hudson told an interviewer that Dean was sulky, ill-mannered, and difficult to work with: "He was always angry and full of contempt. . . . He never smiled."

Whatever difficulties Dean had with Hudson, they paled in comparison to those he experienced with his director. George Stevens considered Dean a brash upstart—talented, perhaps, but too rebellious for his own good. On the first day of shooting, Stevens tried to exercise control by telling Dean exactly where to stand

James Dean, Rock Hudson, and Elizabeth Taylor enjoy a festive moment during the filming of *Giant.* Later, Hudson complained that Dean was a difficult actor to work with: "While doing a scene, in the giving and taking, he was just a taker. He would suck everything out and never give back."

and how to deliver his lines. He knew that Dean would resent his authoritarian approach, but he felt it was important to establish their roles from the outset.

"There's always a testing period in the beginning of a picture when an actor wants to find out who's boss," Stevens said. "Jimmy was predisposed to do a scene as he saw it, and I had my way of doing it." Inevitably, the two ways were not compatible, and Dean's relationship with the director became a bitter clash of wills.

They were unable, for instance, to come to any agreement on the issue of publicity. To generate interest in *Giant,* Stevens encouraged newspaper reporters to visit the Marfa set. By this time, *East of Eden* had become the highest-grossing film in the nation, and many reporters were anxious to write about Dean. The 24-year-old star, however, declined to give interviews. "What counts to the artist," he maintained, "is performance, not publicity." This irritated the executives at Warner, who felt it was an actor's duty to cooperate with the press.

There were other problems, as well. During the first weeks of shooting, Dean was forced to spend many hours each day in his trailer, waiting for Stevens to use him. In the blistering heat, Dean's patience evaporated, and one morning he failed to show up on the set.

Stevens, in a fury, threatened to suspend him, but Dean refused to be intimidated. "This time it was one day," he warned the director, "the next time it's going to be two days, and then you can start counting the weeks." Stevens, who was not used to being challenged, told Dean that he should learn to shoot his own movies, because he, Stevens, would see to it that he never worked in Hollywood again.

The biggest source of conflict between them, however, had to do with characterization. As usual, Dean wanted to dig into his part, to improvise and experiment. His aim was to make Jett Rink as complex and believable as Clem McCarthy, the real-life Texan upon whom the character was based.

But Stevens had other ideas. He was on a tight schedule and had neither the time nor the patience to deal with a willful Method actor. Some of Dean's improvisations showed remarkable insight, but on the whole Stevens preferred to work with seasoned professionals like Taylor and Hudson, who showed up on time, did what they were told, and created a minimum of trouble.

Hedda Hopper was one of the reporters who visited the Marfa set, and one day Dean told her about the problems he was having. Hopper tried to explain to him why it was important to behave professionally, but it was obvious to her that Dean was feeling frustrated and upset.

Though his performance was excellent, he was plagued by self-doubt, and he confessed to Hopper that he was beginning to hate his work. He swore that he would not see *Giant* after it was released.

"It was really depressing," said Nick Ray, "to see the suffering that boy was going through. *Giant* was really draining him, and I hated watching it happen."

Dean's closest companion on the set was 23-year-old Elizabeth Taylor, who later admitted that their friendship was an unlikely one. "At first," she said, "we were very leery of each other. To him, I was just another Hollywood star, all bosom and no brains. To me, he was a would-be intellectual New York Method actor." By the time the cast returned to Burbank, however, the two had become good friends.

"[Dean] was a strange and fascinating man and seemed engulfed in loneliness," said Taylor. "[One night] he came over to our house, and loved our Siamese cats. I knew he wanted something that belonged to him, something of his own, so I gave him a kitten and he cried."

For nearly a year, Dean had been living in a small apartment on Sunset Plaza Drive in Los Angeles ("a wastebasket with walls," he joked). One Saturday, shortly after returning from Marfa, he moved to a comfortable house in nearby Sherman Oaks, which he rented for $250 a month. He neglected, however, to tell the studio that he was moving that day, and when he failed to show up for work Stevens exploded with anger. On Monday morning, in front of the entire company, he reprimanded Dean, calling him difficult, argumentative, and unprofessional. Stevens warned him that if he ever skipped work again he would be fired.

Late one night, feeling frustrated, Dean went to visit Ann Doran, the actress who had played his mother in *Rebel Without a Cause.* He stood in her front yard yelling "Mom, Mom!" until she brought him inside and served

Bick Benedict (Rock Hudson, left) and Jett Rink (James Dean) come to blows in the wine cellar of Rink's new luxury hotel. Dean was unhappy during much of the filming of *Giant*. "I had nothing to grow on," he complained to his friend Eartha Kitt. "I had no support from anyone."

him hot coffee. "He was so lonesome," Doran recalled. "He just didn't know where to go or what to do. He said he had lots of acquaintances but didn't have any close friends. There was nobody he could talk to."

As summer turned to autumn, Dean was anxious to complete his work on *Giant*. His most difficult sequence in the picture was saved for last. Playing a drunk, middle-aged Jett Rink, he was supposed to deliver a rambling speech in an empty banquet room. "It was a very strange scene," Stevens said, "[one] that a lot of actors would have said just couldn't work."

As the young Rink, Dean's performance had been superb, but now, playing a 46-year-old man, he seemed unsure of himself. He rehearsed his speech endlessly, but to no avail—take after take had to be scrapped. Finally, on September 17, he gave what he considered a perfect reading. Stevens was also pleased, though he later claimed that it "was quite an imposition on Jimmy's acting talent to play a mumbling . . . drunken old man."

Throughout this period, Jane Deacy was negotiating a new contract for her client, a six-year, nine-picture deal that would earn Dean nearly $1 million. He had already informed the studio that after completing *Giant* he planned to take a long vacation. "I want to be in Paris before this year is out. . . ." he confided to a friend. "I want to see the great artists—to see Rome—to buy shoes and crazy clothes in Capri. I want to live."

Before Dean could leave the country, Deacy had arranged for him to star in a television production of Ernest Hemingway's short story, "The Battler," scheduled for a mid-October broadcast. *Rebel,* meanwhile, had been shown to a preview audience and the response was extremely favorable. One newspaper reporter, Joe Hyams, did not exaggerate when he called Dean "the hottest young actor in Hollywood."

On Wednesday, September 21, Dean purchased a new sports car, a silver Porsche 550 Spyder. Made of lightweight aluminum, it was a magnificent vehicle, capable of going 150 miles per hour. Dean was extremely proud of it, and one day he drove the Spyder to the studio to show it to his friends and co-workers. Many people were impressed, but there were others who felt strangely uneasy about the car. Actor Alec Guinness, in particular, begged Dean to get rid of it, swearing that if he kept the Porsche he would be killed within a matter of days.

That same week, Marcus and Ortense Winslow arrived from Indiana for a short visit. They brought along Winton's brother, Charlie Nolan Dean, who years earlier had taught young Jimmy to ride his first motorcycle.

According to Ortense, her nephew seemed to be in good spirits. "He showed us the house he had in Sherman Oaks," she recalled, "[a] big hunting lodge kind of place with just one room. We had dinner with him, and he visited with us out at Winton's house, where we were staying. But we didn't stay too long, because it's a long drive back to Fairmount." Dean offered to take Ortense for a ride in his Porsche, but she declined. The car was too low, she told him. It frightened her.

The Winslows and Charlie Dean knew that their nephew was planning to enter a road race in Salinas on the weekend of October 1 and 2. Dean told Charlie he was anxious to find out just how powerful the Spyder really was. "Be careful, Jim," his uncle warned him. "You're sitting on a bomb."

By the end of the week, Dean had convinced three friends to accompany him to Salinas: Bill Hickman, his dialogue coach for *Giant;* Rolf Weutherich, the 28-year-

In a classic American image, James Dean portrays wildcatter Jett Rink.

old German mechanic who had sold him the Porsche a week earlier; and Sanford Roth, a photographer who was shooting a photo essay on Dean for *Collier's* magazine. Roth thought it would be interesting to take a picture of the actor as he crossed the finish line in Salinas.

On Friday morning, September 30, Dean drove the Spyder to Competition Motors, a dealership in Hollywood. There Weutherich checked over the engine, making sure it was ready for Saturday's race. Dean offered to help, but the mechanic waved him aside. "No, thanks," Weutherich said, "you'll only complicate things."

Shortly thereafter, Bill Hickman and Sanford Roth arrived at the garage. Originally, they had all planned to drive to Salinas in a Ford station wagon, towing the Porsche behind on a trailer. It was a beautiful day, however, and at the last minute Dean decided to drive the Spyder instead. "It'll put some miles on the clock and loosen her up," he explained to the others.

It sounded like a reasonable plan, and Weutherich climbed into the Porsche with Dean, who gunned the engine and took off toward the freeway. Hickman and Roth followed behind in the station wagon, towing the empty trailer. After stopping for gas, the two cars headed north on Highway 99 (now Highway 5).

Dean, who was wearing blue pants and a white T-shirt, passed the time by telling jokes and smoking cigarettes. Around three in the afternoon, he and Weutherich stopped at Tip's Diner, where Dean ordered a tall glass of ice-cold milk. "I'd never seen Jimmy so happy," said Weutherich. "He talked and laughed and seemed very at ease." While Dean drank his milk, Weutherich gave him advice about the race in Salinas. "Don't drive to win," he said. "Drive to get experience."

Half an hour later, on a steep grade of highway known as the Grapevine, Dean was pulled over by a patrol car for doing 70 in a 55-MPH zone. Bill Hickman also received a speeding ticket, but he was only trying to keep up with the Porsche.

His enthusiasm only slightly dampened, Dean continued on, turning left onto Route 466 (now 46), a narrow, two-lane highway that would take him to Paso Robles, where he and his companions planned to have dinner. "The road was one gray line, cutting through monotonous landscape. . . ." said Weutherich. "It felt like driving on an endless ruler."

At five o'clock, both drivers stopped at a roadside grocery store, where Sanford Roth bought some apples. Dean made a quick phone call, then hopped back into the Porsche. "Nonstop to Paso Robles!" he shouted, stepping on the accelerator. In his haste, Dean failed to fasten his seat belt.

The sun was beginning to set and Weutherich felt sleepy. He closed his eyes and settled back into his seat. At approximately 5:45 P.M., Dean was approaching the small town of Cholame, where Route 466 intersected with Route 41. The sun was shining into his eyes, but he did not slow down. Impatiently, he zipped past another driver, who estimated that the Spyder was going at least 85 miles per hour.

Dean was nearing the Y-intersection when, up ahead, he noticed a black-and-white Ford Sedan in the opposite, eastbound lane. The driver of the Ford, a 23-year-old student named Donald Turnupseed, was preparing to turn onto Route 41, directly across the westbound lane of 466.

"That guy up there's gotta stop," Dean said to Weutherich. "He'll see us." But Turnupseed saw nothing: The silver Spyder was too low to the ground to be easily visible in the fading light. By the time Dean realized that the Ford was not going to stop, it was too late. A moment later, there was a tremendous crash, a sickening twist of aluminum—and silence.

Hickman and Roth pulled up a few minutes later in the station wagon. They were horrified by what they saw. The Spyder had been slammed into a ditch—according to Roth, it looked like "a crumpled pack of cigarettes." Weutherich was alive, laying face down on the ground nearby. Miraculously, he had been thrown clear of the wreck. Turnupseed, who had suffered only minor bruises, was tearfully describing what had happened to a police officer. "I didn't see him," he kept repeating. "I swear I didn't see him. . . ."

At the moment of impact, Dean's neck had snapped back with such force that his head was nearly severed from his torso. The medical report later revealed he had multiple broken bones and lacerations over his entire body. "The ambulance came. . . ." remembered Roth, who in a daze began taking pictures of the gruesome tragedy. "I begged the attendant to keep Jimmy under oxygen on the way to the hospital, but it was no use. Neither was the 15-mile race against time. . . . Jimmy was dead."

After the tragic crash that cost James Dean his life, the ruined Porsche Spyder was taken around to various schools in the Los Angeles area to encourage teenagers to drive safely.

IN MEMORY OF JAMES DEA

THE FAIRMOUNT NEWS

XXX — Fairmount, Grant County, Indiana — SPECIAL

pecial

f the overwhelm-
for this week's
IE FAIRMOUNT
h contains exclus-
concerning the
career of James
ve sold all of our
s, even though we
al hundred extras.
dy, we decided to
Special Edition to
t the public's de-

nbers of the staff,
o take this oppor-
expressing our
the bereaved fam-
ean. Words can
express emotions
is of time such as
Dean and his
Fairmount will
otten.

N'S "EDEN"
GH TALENT
UNT ACTOR

my Dean weren't
oy, "East of Eden"
of the most power-
ever released by
ers and it would
h the effort and
ne.

Easter Sunday at
ana Theatre and
through Thursday,
ohn DeBoo, Man-

omefolks will be
Dean. And, they
pointed if they are
d a splendid per-
magnificient in-
Jimmy.

star has been com-
n Brando and this
some faint simi-
the two. But,
mer personality..
ects itself with a
tion that keeps
the edge of their

immy plays the
apredictable, love-
who was reared
by their father
sey).

an inferiority
ght about chiefly
ought his father
rother to himself,
oes everything in
'win" his father's

ic scenes, each
mer, are seen in
of the show and
n Dean seems to
soul with his

John Steinbeck,
takes place in the
as section of Cal-
usual with Stein-
en, who produced
e picture, did an
b; but, this is
azan, who is one
foremost produc-

said that there is
mmy will be a
Academy Award
work in "Eden".
e year, though, it
to forecast.
s have seen "East
y place it has
our opinion this
om. Fairmount to

ning the Indiana
a special perfor-
den" for Mrs.
Fairmount High
instructor, who
his way.
with the senior
cials and several
usiastic with the
people who see

Photo by Curtis Bernard, Santa Monica, Calif.

. . . a Student at U.C.L.A.

James Dean

A native son who startled the nation with a brilliant flash of genius was brought back home this week for last rites. His brief career was as bright as a meteor which flows like a golden tear down the dark cheeks of night.

By the law of averages, it was most unusual for a lad 24-years of age to leave a rural environment from an agarian community and go so far and fast in so short a time on Broadway and Hollywood. It is in the grass roots of Grant County from which he made his start that the body of this restless youth has been returned to rest.

He made his living at acting—by his own definition—"behavior of and for other people". For a little period of time he made the lives of many more entertaining, more interesting, and in some cases more bearable. Such a life is not suddenly wiped out in the wreckage of a car in California. Some of us have learned to distrust our senses and to know that as long as we remember, there will live on in our hearts the influence of others.

To be an actor requires a trained memory, the ability to be a severe critic of oneself, and to create moods and atmosphere for the development of that art. James Dean's path, to those of us who knew him best, was steep and rugged and was covered with sandpaper instead of velvet. As he said in a letter to a friend, "we are impaled on a crook of conditioning. A fish that is in the water has no choice that he is. Genius would have it that he swim in sand. We are fish and we drown. We remain in one world and wonder. The fortunate are taught to ask why. No one can answer."

Human life has been compared often to an automobile. Some get more mileage in 30 years than others do in 60. So even though we "weep for the dead, the doubly dead, in that he died so young", yet we feel that Jim who lived dangerously would have had the last act come as it did as last nights must come to all earthly things.

Perhaps he would recite for us, if he could, the lines of a lesser poet, John G. Neihardt who wrote,

"Let me live out my years in heat of blood!
Let me die drunken with the dreamer's wine!
Let me not see this soul-house built of mud
Go toppling to the dust—a vacant shrine!
Let me go quickly like a candle light
Snuffed out just at the heyday of its glow!
Give me high noon—and let it then be night!
Thus would I go.
And grant me, when I face the grisly Thing,
One haughty cry to pierce the gray Perhaps!
O let me be a tune-swept fiddlestring
That feels the Master Melody — and snaps."

JAD

$105,000 ESTATE LEFT BY ACTOR JIMMY DEAN

An estate valued at $105,000, according to court records, was left by James Dean, whose body young actor, is the only direct heir.

Attorney L. Dean Petty filed a petition for letters of administration to Dean's estate Wednesday in Hollywood. The attorney

James Dean Killed As R
Of California Car Accide

FAIRMOUNT IS STUNNED TO LEARN OF TRAGEDY WHICH CLAIMED NATIVE SON; HEADON COLLISION NEAR INTERSECTION CAUSES FATALITY FRIDAY

Fairmount was stunned.

Saturday morning, which was the time most people learned of the violent tragedy that claimed the life of James Dean, the people who knew and loved him best could hardly conceive of the fact.

Death is always a hard thing to understand and especially when it strikes a young person, who apparently has much to give to the world and who is just beginning what could be a brilliant career.

That's how most people look at the accident which killed Jimmy (as he was known to homefolks).

Death came as result of a headon collision last Friday night near Paso Robles, California when the sports car he was driving was struck by another vehicle.

He died en route to the Paso Robles hospital after suffering multiple fractures of both arms and internal injuries.

Ralph Wueterich, 27, Hollywood, Dean's auto mechanic, was seriously injured. Donald Turnupseed, 23, Tulare, Calif., driver of the other car, escaped with minor injuries.

According to the California State Patrol, Turnupseed's car turned left from a road onto the highway where Jimmy was driving and the smash-up occured.

Warner Brothers, who owned his contract, had told Jimmy not to drive his sports car, a Porsche Spyder, while working on a picture. However, he had just finished "Giant" at its Texas location a few days beforehand.

Reportedly, he was traveling to an amateur car race.

Jimmy was born in Fairmount, the son of Mr. and Mrs. Winton Dean, on February 8, 1931. They lived here five years from that time when they moved to Santa Monica, Calif.

His mother, the former Mildred Wilson, died in 1940 when Jimmy was nine-years-old.

He then came to live with his uncle and aunt, Mr. and Mrs. Marcus Winslow, and graduated from Fairmount High School in 1949.

Following his high school graduation, Jimmy enrolled at the University of City of Los Angeles. Then he left college and went to New York City where he was cast in minor TV rolls on, "Studio One", "You Are There" and "Television Playhouse".

As result of his television acting, Jimmy was cast in the Broadway play, "The Immoralist", and ultimately won the David Blum award for the most promising stage newcomer.

Elia Kazan, famed Hollywood director, caught Jimmy's performance on Broadway and signed him to play Caleb in "East of Eden", based on John Steinbeck's novel.

Jimmy shot to stardom with almost unbelievable rapidity as result of his work in "Eden". Homefolks who saw the movie were heard to comment that many of the mannerisms Jimmy used were just like he did "at home".

Mrs. Adeline Nall, former Fairmount High School teacher, first started Jimmy on his road to success as she recognized his ability and tutored and encouraged him to develop it.

"That spontaneous laugh" Mrs. Nall said after seeing "East of Eden", "was so very natural. It was one of his traits I'd noticed

Press, said, "Dean could well become Hollywood's first posthumous Academy Award winner for his role in "East of Eden".

Many critics have credited Jimmy's debut in the movie as the male Oscar performance to beat.

"Dean was the hottest property we had," a Warner Brothers official said. "We had great plans for him".

George Stevens, who directed "Giant", said Jimmy's death was "a great tragedy. He had extraordinary talent."

Comments like this could go on and on for it was generally conceeded that James Dean was "something special" . . . and he was "something special" to his home town, too, forgetting his achievements in movieland.

During high school days, Jimmy was extremely active in extra curricular work. His portrayal of "the monster" in a high school version of "Frankenstein" will be recalled by many.

. . . Basketball Star

Hackett Studio

Then too, he was a member of the ever-popular basketball team representing the Quakers from Fairmount High. During his senior year in the sectional tourney he shot a last-second field goal to beat Gas City 39-37.

In addition he was a member of the track and baseball teams and was awarded the school's top athlete medal his last year in high school at which time he was also given the art department medal.

Perhaps among the first signs of his dramatic talent came while he was a youngster and won silver and gold medals in WCTU speaking contests.

In 1949, his senior year in high school, Jimmy won first place for acting during the National Forensic League's state contest at Peru.

Outside of his school activities, many people will remember Jimmy ice skating on the Winslow pond just North of Fair-

Each time that he came home for a visit he would also visit the high school and talk to the student body. On one occasion he explained the art of bull fighting . . . which he had practiced somewhat.

On his last visit he arrived in time to attend a dance at the high school and during the evening he played the drums . . . mambo fashion.

Magazines galore have given valuable publicity space to the "Indiana farm boy" who had risen to a Hollywood star in such a short time. LIFE magazine even sent a photographer to Fairmount with Jimmy to get shots of him in his home surroundings.

(Copies of the magazine were sold before they arrived at the newsstands and are at a premium today.)

Just a few days before his death a Sunday supplement in

one of the la
this area car
ing with the
in Texas.

It went int
how the hea
of all the acto
is, except J
would go ra
evening.

Jimmy Dea
in the 24 sho
great many
understand h
eccentric. Pe
then again,
comes so wr
thing he f
else but that
When he l
apt to be ou
bounds of act
the measure o
His home
him, though.
And they'll

Last Rites Wi
Held Here Sat

Dr. James A. DeWeerd, Rev. Xen Harvey To Conduct

Funeral services for James Dean, 24, will be held at 2 o'clock Saturday afternoon at the Friends Church in Fairmount by Dr. James A. DeWeerd and the Rev. Xen Harvey, pastor of the church.

Dr. DeWeerd, who has a telecast at Cincinnati shortly before services begin at 2 o'clock, will be flown in the private plane of Buford Cadle to Marion Airport and is scheduled to arrive there at 1:45.

He will be met by a State Police Patrol car and be driven to the Friends Church.

Following the church service, burial will take place at Park Cemetery in Fairmount.

The Rev. Xen Harvey said Thursday night that his church will accomodate approximately 600 people by adding extra chairs. In addition to the ampli-

fying system a
public addres
enable those
rites.

Wilbur Hun
Funeral Home
arrangements,
ceived reques
that seats be r

Hunt said
denied in vie
this is to be a

A Hunt Fu
bulance met t
young Dean's
fornia at 10:1
the Indianapo

The body w
Funeral Hom
may call.

Survivors i
Winton Dean,
ternal grandfa
Marion; pate
Mr. and Mrs
Fairmount; Ch
uncle, Gas Ci
Mrs. Marcus W
aunt, Fairmou

DEATH OF JAMES DEAN, FAIRMOUNT CASTS A PALL OF SADNESS OVER S

The shocking news of the death of James Dean has cast a spell of unbelievable saddness over Fairmount High School. The graduate of the class of '49 had soared to fame in his first picture "East of Eden" and had just completed two more pictures. The students, faculty, and townspeople have all been very proud of his great accomplishments in such a short time.

Jimmie's family had just spent a month with him in California and were on their way home when the fatal accident occured. The Winslows arrived home early Monday evening only then to learn of the tragic car accident which killed Jim just one week ago today.

The students feel they knew Jim well, because he spoke before them in convocations whenever he was home and visited many of the classrooms especially speech classes. Because he was a Fairmount graduate the students felt especially proud when he came back to the

Jim did eve
intense desire
he liked a
seemed to be w
had. Racing,
drums were th
this intensity.
from others, m
teresting perso
different, but
all his own.

Commentato
have stated th
liant career ahe
picture he ga
that usually t
a long time to

Cards of sym
ed into the
family from a
States. It is ap
many, many fr
actresses he ha
expected to at
The final fur
held tomorrow
Friends Church

Fairmount's

9 A Boy Named Jimmy Dean

On the evening of Friday, September 30, 1955, George Stevens, Rock Hudson, and Elizabeth Taylor were in a projection room at Warner Brothers watching footage from *Giant* when the phone rang. Stevens answered it. As he listened to the voice at the other end, his face went white. Putting down the receiver, he ordered the projectionist to stop the film.

"I have an announcement to make," he said, in a shaken voice. "Jimmy Dean has been killed." Elizabeth Taylor collapsed in her seat, grief-stricken. Later that evening, in the parking lot, she told Stevens that she could not believe Dean was dead. Stevens's reply was caustic: "I believe it. The way he drove, he had it coming."

The tragic news spread quickly through Hollywood; from there it filtered out across the nation. The Winslows, who were driving back to Fairmount, heard something on the car radio about the death of a young actor, but they paid little attention. It was not until they reached the farm that they learned, to their horror, that it was Jimmy. Ortense burst into tears.

One week after the death of James Dean, the *Fairmount News* published a special edition entirely devoted to his memory.

Among Dean's acquaintances, there were many who believed that his death was inevitable, that sooner or later his reckless approach to life would result in tragedy. In New York, Dean's former girlfriend, Barbara Glenn, accepted the news with quiet resignation. "I don't think on that particular day he set out to commit suicide," she later said. "I never expected him to get on his bike and say, 'I'm never coming back.' But I knew it was imminent. . . . Sure, that day it was an accident. Just like any other day it would have been an accident."

On Monday, October 3, Dean's body was flown from California to Indiana. The funeral was held five days later, on Saturday, October 8. Three thousand people attended the services, which were held at Back Creek Friends Church in Fairmount. After the funeral, Dean was taken

In October 1956, one year after Dean's death, a memorial service was held at Park Cemetery in Fairmount.

to nearby Park Cemetery, where he was buried beneath a simple granite headstone.

The Winslows were naturally stunned by what had happened, but they tried to remember the good and always spoke warmly of their talented nephew. "There'll never be another boy like him," Ortense told the press.

A few days before leaving for Salinas, Dean had taken out a $100,000 accidental death insurance policy. He was also planning to draw up a will, leaving $85,000 to his aunt and uncle. In the absence of a will, however, the court awarded Dean's entire estate to his father, Winton. The Winslows received nothing.

On October 26, 1955, *Rebel Without a Cause* premiered at the Astor Theater in New York. "As a starring vehicle for Dean," said one reviewer, "[the film] is satisfactory, giving the late, lamented young actor a role similar to the one he had in . . . *East of Eden*. And with complete control of the character, he gives a fine, sensitive performance of an unhappy, lonely teenager, tormented by the knowledge of his emotional instability."

There was one sequence in *Rebel* that fascinated and disturbed everyone. To "prove" their masculinity, Jim Stark and another teenager, Buzz, drive a pair of stolen cars at full speed toward the edge of a cliff. The first boy to leap to safety is a coward, a "chickie." At the last moment, Buzz gets his jacket sleeve caught on the door handle and, unable to escape, plunges over the cliff. Critics were quick to point out that Dean's recent death gave the sequence "an almost unbearable morbid ring."

Rebel Without a Cause proved extremely popular with teenagers, who flocked to see it in ever-increasing numbers. They identified with the character of Jim Stark, who in their minds somehow merged with the person of James Dean. With uncanny accuracy, Dean mirrored the frustrations and confusions they, too, were feeling. He attacked the conformity and hypocrisy of their parents' generation and, by doing so, suggested a more honest (if more painful) approach to life. "In James Dean," wrote filmmaker François Truffaut, "today's youth discovers itself."

As many writers and sociologists have observed, the time was right for the advent of James Dean. Rock and roll was just about to come into fashion; like Dean, it would symbolize a radical departure from the past, a reckless, passionate embrace of the here and now. As Truffaut saw it, Dean represented a number of important aspects of adolescence: "continual fantasy life, . . . eternal [teenage] love of tests and trials, . . . regret at feeling oneself 'outside' society, . . . and, finally, acceptance—or refusal—of the world as it is."

American teenagers identified so strongly with Dean (and Jim Stark) that they began to imitate the violence they had seen at fictional Dawson High. Switchblade fights broke out, and in some communities teenagers stole cars and tried to recreate the "chickie run," sometimes with tragic results.

Soon, the same thing was happening overseas, and *Rebel Without a Cause* came to be regarded as a social nuisance by some public officials. The picture was censored in England and banned altogether in Japan, Spain, and Mexico. Screenwriter Stewart Stern took a trip around the world after the film's release, and he was astounded by the impact the movie was having in foreign countries.

"Wherever [I] went," he said, "people would come up and start talking about *Rebel.* There was one boy in the Philippines who could speak no English at all, but he had memorized the entire screenplay. I met his parents, and they said he was *crazed* with this movie. . . . And apparently that was the general experience, that the kids found that movie wherever it was allowed. *Parents would be taken to that film by their children.* It was as if the children

were saying, 'I can't say this to you, but this is really what I mean.'"

By early 1956, Warner Brothers had received thousands of letters from distraught fans, many of whom refused to believe that their idol was dead. "Dear Jimmy," one girl wrote, "all this remembrance stuff is a waste of time, because I know you are still alive. Why worry so much about the way you look, because your fans worship you however disfigured you are."

Somehow, the rumor got started that Dean was secretly recuperating on the Warner lot. A large crowd of frenzied teenagers showed up at the studio gate, waving photographs and shrieking their love. At last, Warner Brothers was forced to turn down all requests for information relating to their dead star, claiming they did not "want to encourage or exploit this morbid interest in him."

Rebel Without a Cause presented the turbulent lives of a group of high school students. The film was very popular with teenagers, who identified strongly with Dean's character, Jim Stark. "In *Rebel*," writes one biographer, "Jimmy plays himself. He is both victim and hero, and he injects the film with all the diffuse fragments of his own personality."

Many of the fans who wrote to the studio also sent money, and on May 15, 1956, the James Dean Memorial Foundation was established in Fairmount, Indiana. The purpose of the nonprofit organization was to keep alive the memory of Dean, to provide scholarships and financial assistance to gifted young artists, and to promote through education "the dramatic, musical, and literary arts and sciences." (After a lengthy period of financial disarray, the foundation was successfully reorganized in the 1980s. Today it vigorously protects the image of James Dean, which has become a highly profitable merchandising symbol.)

Though Dean's death had set off a global frenzy among young people, there were many adults at the time who viewed the situation with a more cynical eye. In the *Detroit Free Press,* writer Maurice Zolotow suggested that it was morally unhealthy for teenagers to idolize "a second-rate actor" like Dean: "Why should we shed maudlin tears and slobber over the memory of such a man? What's so brave and beautiful about stepping on the gas, blowing your horn and speeding down a public highway like a maniac? . . . Jimmy Dean was rotten all the way down the line."

The Italian press agreed, observing that the "infatuation for James Dean is the direct result of a grave state of anguish that exists among the adolescents in America and elsewhere."

But the worldwide obsession with Dean continued unabated. It was, in fact, the most extraordinary outburst of hysteria over a movie star since the 1926 death of Rudolph Valentino. In Hamburg, Germany, two teenage girls committed suicide, unable to face life without the presence of James Dean. Many women in America claimed to be pregnant with Dean's baby, and a postman in England who had seen *Rebel* 400 times had his name legally changed to James Byron Dean. Happily, he told reporters that he was now "controlled by the spirit of the late actor."

Fan clubs, meanwhile, had formed throughout the world. The largest was the James Dean Memory Ring, centered in New York. Every week, members would gather to light candles, listen to classical music, and talk in hushed tones about their idol. Some of Dean's more ardent fans performed ceremonies that were mystical, even semireligious, in nature. By doing so, they hoped in some way to connect with Dean's spirit. "Many young people had no emotional roots and were without a basic faith," said John Steinbeck's former wife, Gwin. "Dean became a substitute Christ. As such, they even tried to resurrect him."

On a simpler level, the death of James Dean served to unite young people. They understood and identified with his anger, his confusion, and his feeling of always being an outsider. By keeping Dean alive in their conversations and their quasi-religious ceremonies, they were unconsciously helping each other pass from the turbulence of adolescence to the calmer maturity of adulthood.

"The adoration and virtual canonization of the late James Dean continues to mushroom," wrote one reporter. "It is one of the phenomena of this celebrity-worshipping era that future anthropologists may study with deep interest."

To feed the public's insatiable hunger for anything relating to Dean, a number of pop records were released: "Jimmy, Jimmy," "The Ballad of James Dean," "Hymn for James Dean," "Jimmy Dean's First Christmas in Heaven," and "A Boy Named Jimmy Dean." There were look-alike contests, bubble gum cards, James Dean rings, medallions, "Miracleflesh" masks, "authentic" locks of Dean's hair, buttons, switchblade knives ("The James

Natalie Wood and James Dean appear here in a scene from *Rebel.* Dean's three films for Warner Brothers continue to enjoy brisk sales, and new Dean biographies are published regularly. As one writer recently observed, "Young people everywhere are rediscovering James Dean: his appeal is universal."

Dean Special"), and pieces of broken glass and twisted aluminum said to have been taken from the wrecked Porsche Spyder.

Hundreds of articles appeared in fan magazines, many of which deliberately adopted a macabre or sensational tone: "Jimmy Dean Fights Back from the Grave," "The Legend of James Dean," "The Man They Won't Let Die," "You Can Make Jimmy Dean Live Forever." A 35-cent magazine that purported to reveal Dean's "own words from the Beyond" sold an astonishing 500,000 copies. Dean's former roommate, Bill Bast, wrote a book about his friend that was published in 1956, the first of a long line of James Dean biographies.

As fans became acquainted with the details of Dean's life, thousands of people began to descend on the small town of Fairmount, eager to see the sights of Dean's boyhood and to talk to the people who had known him. Marcus and Ortense Winslow were forever giving interviews and patiently answering questions about their nephew.

"There'd always be somebody at the door," said Marcus, "who'd been to the cemetery to visit Jim and wanted to spend a bit of time with us. We thought it would end after a while. We thought that Jim would be left to rest quietly, but we should have known better. All his life, Jim always did the opposite of whatever we expected of him."

On October 10, 1956, one year after Dean's death, *Giant* opened at the Roxy Theater in New York. "A virtuoso performance by Dean," said one reviewer, "whose Jett Rink is a willful, brilliant variation on the character he made his own and died for—the baffled, tender, violent adolescent rejected by the world he rejects."

The *New York Herald-Tribune* also raved about Dean's acting, calling Jett Rink "the most memorable character in *Giant*. Devotees of the cult which has grown up around [Dean] since he was killed . . . may be somewhat surprised to see him slouching around in dark glasses and a pencil-thin mustache as the dissipated hotel and oil tycoon in the latter stages of the film. But his earlier depiction of the amoral, reckless, animal-like young ranch hand will not only excite his admirers to frenzy, it will make the most sedate onlooker understand why a James Dean cult ever came into existence."

Giant was an extremely popular movie, taking in $14 million at the box office. For Dean's fans, however, it remains the least satisfying of his three pictures. Despite its epic intentions, it succeeds only fitfully as a multigenerational saga; the character of Jett Rink is never fully developed; and, in the opinion of many critics, the final banquet scene is unconvincing.

"Dean had no technique to speak of," said director Elia Kazan. "When he tried to play an older man in the last reels of *Giant,* he looked like what he was: a beginner. On my film, Jimmy would either get the scene right immediately, without any detailed direction—that was 95 percent of the time—or he couldn't get it at all."

In 1956, Dean was nominated for an Academy Award for his performance in *East of Eden.* (Contrary to lore, it was *not* the first time the Academy had nominated a performer posthumously.) A year later, in 1957, Dean was again nominated for his performance in *Giant.* On neither occasion did he win the Oscar. However, he did receive important film awards in France, England, Belgium, Finland, and Japan. According to a spokesman for the James Dean Foundation, his popularity is as strong in foreign countries as it is in the United States: "In a homogenous society like Japan, they admire rebels. In England, his appeal is from nostalgia. And the French think he is sexy."

Most critics agree that James Dean has left a permanent mark on the history of motion pictures. Like Marlon Brando, he introduced an entirely new style of acting that took people by surprise. "Raw, intuitive, and alive," said one writer, "[Brando and Dean] were like unstoppable forces of nature. They seemed more real, more private and neurotic than any actors had ever seemed before. . . . Theirs was acting that had both unexpected size and immediacy, and the risks they took required us to take some risks of our own. . . . How was it possible to absorb [their] performances and not to peer, however fleetingly, into some of our own dark, unsuspected places?"

In *East of Eden* and *Rebel Without a Cause,* Dean established himself as one of the most potent and unconventional actors ever to step before a camera. He aggressively rewrote the rules about how leading men should behave on-screen. By freely exposing his anguish, Dean

"To me," Dean once said to Bill Bast, "the only success, the only greatness for man, is immortality. To have your work remembered in history, to leave something in this world that will last for centuries. That's greatness."

forced audiences to confront their own feelings of alienation and isolation. For this reason, he was, and still is, a controversial star. Many adults in the 1950s found it easiest to dismiss his on-screen torments as nothing but demented playacting, extremist behavior that had little to do with the reality of most American teenagers.

As time passed, however, more and more people began to recognize the fundamental truth of what Dean was trying to say. By the late 1960s, an entire generation of young people had begun to question authority and to embrace new ideas concerning racial pride and sexual identity. They were also sharing feelings of protest and anger, intensified by America's involvement in the Vietnam War. In the light of this new restlessness, James Dean seemed more contemporary than ever. Clad in jeans and a leather jacket, a cigarette dangling defiantly from his lips, he seemed to capture the rebellious spirit of the age, just as he had done a decade earlier.

In his book *A Method to Their Madness: A History of the Actors Studio,* author Foster Hirsch writes that Dean's death in September 1955 "froze him in time at the exact midpoint of the decade. His tragic fate has cast him forever in the role of the brooding fifties rebel crying out against the bland conformity-ridden world he has unwillingly inherited from his elders. . . . As his films recede in time, Dean himself continues to connect to new generations of teenagers. Aspects of his movies may date, but *he* continues to seem real."

There are several reasons for Dean's enduring popularity: the nostalgia he evokes, his sex appeal, and the generally high quality of the three films in which he appeared. The violent manner of his death also holds a grisly fascination for many of his fans. But the primary reason that people continue to talk about Dean is because he was an outstandingly talented actor, tortured and intense, but also surprisingly gentle and soft-spoken. He was dedicated to his craft and, had he lived longer, might well have gone on to become one of the country's most important and influential actors.

In his private life, Dean never managed to find the happiness he sought—and this, too, constitutes part of his universal appeal. He was the eternal loner, seeking but never finding the companionship and love he so desperately desired. In the end, the only constant in Dean's life was his work, which he approached with love, respect, and fierce commitment.

"Being an actor is the loneliest thing in the world," he once told a reporter. "The stage is like a religion; you dedicate yourself to it and suddenly you find that you don't have time to see friends, and it's hard for them to understand. You don't see anybody. You're all alone with your concentration and your imagination and that's all you have. You're an actor."

Appendix ★ ★ ★ ★ ★ ★ ★ ★ ★ ★ ★ ★ ★ ★ ★ ★ ★

Films of James Dean

East of Eden, Warner Brothers, 1955 (directed by Elia Kazan; 115 minutes)
Costarring: Julie Harris, Raymond Massey, Richard Davalos, Jo Van
Fleet, Burl Ives

Rebel Without a Cause, Warner Brothers, 1955 (directed by Nicholas Ray;
111 minutes)
Costarring: Natalie Wood, Jim Backus, Sal Mineo, Ann Doran, Dennis
Hopper, Corey Allen, Nick Adams

Giant, Warner Brothers, 1956 (directed by George Stevens; 198 minutes)
Costarring: Elizabeth Taylor, Rock Hudson, Mercedes McCambridge,
Sal Mineo, Carroll Baker, Chill Wills, Dennis Hopper

James Dean also had bit parts in the following films:

Fixed Bayonets, Twentieth Century-Fox, 1951 (directed by Samuel Fuller;
92 minutes)

Sailor Beware, Paramount, 1951 (directed by Hal Walker; 108 minutes)

Has Anybody Seen My Gal?, Universal, 1952 (directed by Douglas Sirk;
89 minutes)

Trouble Along the Way, Warner Brothers, 1953 (directed by Michael Curtiz;
110 minutes)

Further Reading ★ ★ ★ ★ ★ ★ ★ ★ ★ ★ ★ ★ ★ ★ ★

Adams, Leith, and Keith Burns, eds. *James Dean: Behind the Scenes.* New York: Birch Lane Press, 1990.

Beath, Warren Newton. *The Death of James Dean.* New York: Grove Press, 1986.

Bluttman, Susan. "Rediscovering James Dean: The TV Legacy." *Emmy,* October 1990.

Dalton, David. *James Dean: The Mutant King.* San Francisco: Straight Arrow Books, 1974.

Dalton, David, and Roy Cayen. *James Dean: American Icon.* New York: St. Martin's Press, 1984.

Ferber, Edna. *Giant.* New York: Doubleday, 1952.

Garfield, David. *The Actors Studio: A Player's Place.* New York: Collier Macmillan, 1984.

Gilmore, Jonathan. *The Real James Dean.* New York: Pyramid Books, 1975.

Herndon, Venable. *James Dean: A Short Life.* Garden City, New York: Doubleday, 1974.

Hoskyns, Barney. *James Dean: Shooting Star.* New York: Doubleday, 1989.

Hyams, Joe, with Jay Hyams. *James Dean: Little Boy Lost.* New York: Warner Books, 1992.

Kazan, Elia. *A Life.* New York: Knopf, 1988.

Riese, Randall. *The Unabridged James Dean.* Chicago: Contemporary Books, 1991.

Schatt, Roy. *James Dean: A Portrait.* New York: Ruggles de Latour, 1982.

Steinbeck, John. *East of Eden.* New York: Viking, 1952.

Stock, Dennis. *James Dean Revisited.* New York: Viking Press and Penguin Books, 1978.

Chronology ★ ★ ★ ★ ★ ★ ★ ★ ★ ★ ★ ★ ★ ★ ★ ★

1931	Born James Byron Dean on February 8 in Marion, Indiana
1936	Dean family moves to Santa Monica, California
1940	Mildred Dean dies of cancer on July 14; James Dean returns with his grandmother to live in Fairmount, Indiana
1949	Dean graduates from Fairmount High School on May 16; moves to Santa Monica in June
1950	Enrolls as pre-law student at Santa Monica City College in January; transfers to University of California at Los Angeles in the fall
1951	Appears in Pepsi commercial and televised drama, "Hill Number One"; makes several short movie appearances; moves to New York in September; hired in November as stuntman for CBS's "Beat the Clock"
1952	Accepted as member at Actors Studio; the drama *See the Jaguar* opens at the Cort Theater in New York on December 3 and closes on December 6 after five performances
1953	Dean makes numerous television appearances
1954	The play *The Immoralist* opens at the Royale Theater in New York on February 8; Dean wins a Daniel Blum Theater World Award; gives his final performance on February 23; arrives in Hollywood on March 8 to film *East of Eden*; *East of Eden* begins shooting on May 27 and finishes shooting on August 13

1955   Dean makes trip to New York City and Fairmount, Indiana, in February; *Rebel Without a Cause* begins shooting in March; *Giant* begins shooting in May; Dean purchases a Porsche 550 Spyder on September 21; finishes shooting *Giant* on September 22; is killed in auto accident on September 30 near Cholame, California

1956   James Dean Memorial Foundation established in May to promote "the dramatic, musical, and literary arts and sciences"

Index ★★★★★★★★★★★★★★★★★★★★★★★★★

Alan Schroeder is the author of three other Chelsea House biographies: *Josephine Baker, Jack London,* and *Booker T. Washington.* He is also the author of *Ragtime Tumpie,* an acclaimed account of Josephine Baker's childhood in St. Louis. Selected as one of the Best Books of the Year by *Parents* magazine and the *Boston Globe, Ragtime Tumpie* was also named a Notable Children's Book of 1989 by the American Library Association. Schroeder lives in Alameda, California.

ACKNOWLEDGMENTS
The author dedicates this book to his grandmother, Elizabeth Henningsen, with much love and affection.

Leeza Gibbons is a reporter for and cohost of the nationally syndicated television program "Entertainment Tonight" and NBC's daily talk show "John & Leeza from Hollywood." A graduate of the University of South Carolina's School of Journalism, Gibbons joined the on-air staff of "Entertainment Tonight" in 1984 after cohosting WCBS-TV's "Two on the Town" in New York City. Prior to that, she cohosted "PM Magazine" on WFAA-TV in Dallas, Texas, and on KFDM-TV in Beaumont, Texas. Gibbons also hosts the annual "Miss Universe," "Miss U.S.A.," and "Miss Teen U.S.A." pageants, as well as the annual Hollywood Christmas Parade. She is active in a number of charities and has served as the national chairperson for the Spinal Muscular Atrophy Division of the Muscular Dystrophy Association; each September, Gibbons cohosts the National MDA Telethon with Jerry Lewis.